T0353650

THE LIFE THAT MATTERS

MANIFESTO

THE 11 PRINCIPLES TO KNOW AND COMMIT TO LIVE A LIFE THAT MATTERS

ADAM LANDRUM

BALBOA.PRESS
A DIVISION OF HAY HOUSE

Copyright © 2024 Adam Landrum.

All rights reserved. No part of this book may be used or reproduced by any means,
graphic, electronic, or mechanical, including photocopying, recording, taping or by
any information storage retrieval system without the written permission of the author
except in the case of brief quotations embodied in critical articles and reviews.

Balboa Press books may be ordered through booksellers or by contacting:

Balboa Press
A Division of Hay House
1663 Liberty Drive
Bloomington, IN 47403
www.balboapress.com
844-682-1282

Because of the dynamic nature of the Internet, any web addresses or links contained
in this book may have changed since publication and may no longer be valid. The views
expressed in this work are solely those of the author and do not necessarily reflect the
views of the publisher, and the publisher hereby disclaims any responsibility for them.

The author of this book does not dispense medical advice or prescribe the use
of any technique as a form of treatment for physical, emotional, or medical
problems without the advice of a physician, either directly or indirectly. The
intent of the author is only to offer information of a general nature to help you
in your quest for emotional and spiritual well-being. In the event you use any
of the information in this book for yourself, which is your constitutional right,
the author and the publisher assume no responsibility for your actions.

Any people depicted in stock imagery provided by Getty Images are models,
and such images are being used for illustrative purposes only.
Certain stock imagery © Getty Images.

Scripture quotations are taken from the Holy Bible, New Living Translation,
copyright © 1996, 2004, 2015 by Tyndale House Foundation. Used by permission of
Tyndale House Publishers Inc., Carol Stream, Illinois 60188. All rights reserved.

Print information available on the last page.

ISBN: 979-8-7652-5561-2 (sc)
ISBN: 979-8-7652-5562-9 (e)

Library of Congress Control Number: 2024919381

•

Balboa Press rev. date: 10/07/2024

Dedicated To:

My wife Shely,
for being my biggest cheerleader,
and being the best example of a person that
lives a Life That Matters.

Contents

Wired to Matter

Introduction

We're starving to matter. From the moment we're born, we seek love and affection. As toddlers, we demand attention. Soon, we desire to be the teacher's pet, feeling gratified when chosen to help with a meaningless and monotonous chore. We play hard in sports, striving to impress our friends, coaches, parents, a few kids we like—and even those we don't. Strange, isn't it? At work, we crave recognition, appreciation, and the titles and raises that accompany them. We search for love, and most of us pursue marriage, hoping to love and value someone as much as they love and value us. Then the cycle continues as we take on the privilege of raising children, helping them discover their own sense of what it means to matter.

We desperately want our lives to matter to ourselves.

But that's not enough. Along the journey of life, we occasionally face existential crises: Why am I here? Why do I exist? Do I matter in the grand scheme of life? Each of us wrestles with our own versions of these questions, finding our own answers. Sometimes, we feel like we matter a great deal. At other times, we feel as though we don't matter at all. It's maddening.

We are wired to matter, and nothing feels better than truly believing we do. Most people have the potential to matter much more than they realize. I wrote this book to encourage those courageous enough to want to matter—whether it's a whole lot more or just a little bit more.

The truth is, you matter very much. And if you don't believe that, keep reading, because you'll discover that you do. This book will provide you with the concepts and language to define and articulate what truly matters to you through the Life That Matters Manifesto. I've included tools to help you craft your manifesto, which you can refer to throughout your life to maintain and grow your Life That Matters. I'm excited for the self-discovery journey you're about to embark on. If I can be of any assistance, please feel free to reach out to me—I've provided my contact information at the back of the book.

Adam Landrum
Greenville, South Carolina

SECTION 1

Two Lives, Different Matterings

To provide some context for living a Life That Matters, let's explore the lives of two fictional characters and see to what extent they are living lives that matter.

Bob

Bob is recently divorced and estranged from his kids. He goes to work, but he's not engaged; it's just a job to him. He does his job adequately, but almost anyone could replace him.

He gives very little of himself—neither serving in the community nor contributing money or resources. His days are largely consumed by a two-hour round-trip commute, eight hours at work, and the rest of his time spent eating, drinking, or on a screen, consuming social media, news, TV shows, and some porn. Whatever time is left is for sleep, which isn't enough.

Bob is unhappy. He's obese, though he thinks he's just overweight. On weekends, he sleeps in, does the bare minimum around his apartment, and spends even more time on his devices. He doesn't have deep friendships; in fact, he doesn't have friends at all. Bob is understandably lonely and anxious, and he struggles with depression. He never drank much before, but he's noticed his drinking has increased. It's now a daily habit, with an average of three alcoholic drinks a day. His unspoken nightly goal is a solid buzz, if not a little drunk.

For Bob, life feels like Phil's in *Groundhog Day*. Each day and night are the same. He's miserable, lonely, and bored out of his mind. Every night, he goes to sleep and wakes up to do it all over again. He can't help but wonder, "Why am I doing this? Does any of this matter? Do I even matter?"

In a nutshell, that's Bob's life. What do you think? How much does Bob's life matter?

Reading about Bob's life is a little like watching reality television. Seeing how messed up other people's lives are makes us feel just a little bit better about ourselves, doesn't it? "At least I'm not like that," we think. But mattering by comparison is not the goal. The objective isn't to matter more than others; it's to ensure that our lives matter to ourselves.

Maybe the life I described in Bob's story is exactly the one you're living, and you can totally relate. Or perhaps you're on the opposite end of the spectrum and can't even imagine a life like Bob's. Or can you?

Although Bob's story is fictitious, it's roughly based on the statistical probability of what an average American male's life might look like. Statistically, "Bob" is more likely to be divorced, be a heavy drinker, be overweight, be disengaged at work, not spend enough time with his kids, and spend most of his free time on screens.

It seems that Bob isn't living much of a Life That Matters—much like millions of others, statistically speaking, in the United States and around the world.

###

Mark

Mark is happily married with three kids and absolutely loves his job. As a physical therapist, he is passionate about helping people recover from injuries and return to a healthy lifestyle.

He and his wife chose to live close to his office for a short 10-minute commute, and they strategically picked a neighborhood full of kids and couples their age. They've made great friends, and so have their kids. The schools are excellent, and they're also just 10 minutes from their church, where they are very involved.

Mark loves to run and plays golf every Thursday evening in a league with his friends. He has a handful of close friends he regularly sees and spends time with. Mark also looks forward to his weekly date night with his wife, and the family plays golf together a couple of times a month.

Mark is passionate about the environment and has gone as green as possible, practically speaking. He also volunteers in his community, helping with trash pickup in parks and streams. Additionally, he mentors students in a physical therapy program, guiding them as they launch their careers.

Together, Mark and his wife lead a marriage ministry to help couples with troubled marriages. They are planning to write a marriage book and speak at conferences. They envision, God willing, impacting thousands—if not tens of thousands—of marriages.

Mark loves his kids, but more importantly, his kids love him! He takes them to school every morning, joking that he has a captive audience. Since time with the kids isn't as much as he'd like, he makes sure the family has sit-down dinners five times a week. Mark also prioritizes family vacations, organizing two big trips a year and one smaller long-weekend trip to the lake.

MARK

Mark doesn't watch TV because he simply doesn't have the time. Even if he did, he'd prefer to read. He goes to bed early so he can wake up early to run, read, meditate, and pray—before having breakfast with his family, taking the kids to school, and heading to work to see his first patient.

That's Mark. You kind of want to punch him in the throat, don't you? He's that perfect, leave-it-to-beaver type. And yes, he is. Mark knows what's important to him and has made deliberate choices to align his activities with what matters. He's clear about what he wants and where he's going, and he ensures that nearly all his energy is directed toward that. He's also constantly cutting out unimportant things that waste time and energy.

Mark believes in something and someone bigger than himself. He's passionate about a cause, values serving others, and gives generously of his time, talents, and treasures. Mark has purpose in his life and a vision to live in a way that helps others.

Moreover, Mark knows what matters to him and his family, which allows him to make decisions based on those priorities. Yes, he has discipline. Yes, he's lived a life that's generated little baggage, like debt or failed relationships, which can drain so much energy from a person, but not Mark.

Mark is fortunate, but he's also smart. You have to give him credit for creating an *exquisite* life for himself—it's hard to blame him for how he's chosen to live.

Mark has created and is living a Life That Matters.

1

Levels of Mattering

Do you matter, or are you just surviving?

Rocks exist. A squirrel survives. You matter. But what does it mean to matter?

"To matter" involves the qualities that set you apart from every other organic or inorganic thing in the universe. Unlike things that merely exist, you have the ability to operate based on a set of values; to have a purpose and align your life with it. You can identify passions that lie deep within you, and when you honor those passions, you come alive. That is what it means to matter. Mattering is believing in yourself. Mattering is committing. Mattering is living.

For simplicity's sake, there are three levels of living a Life that Matters:

1. Mattering to Yourself
2. Mattering to Others
3. Mattering to God

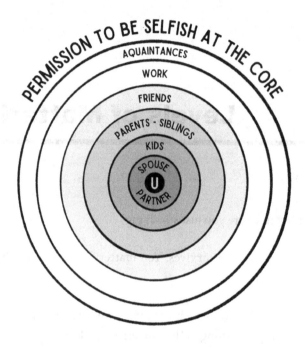

This book primarily focuses on Level 1: Mattering to yourself. When you matter to yourself, you can matter to others. It's about not wasting the amazing gifts you've been given—your body, your brain, your heart, and yes, your soul. You are an incredible creation, and doubting that you matter, even for a second, is just plain ludicrous. But it's also quite normal. We doubt ourselves all the time—some of us daily, if not hourly, if not constantly. My hope is that this book and the Life That Matters Manifesto model will help you discover and convince yourself that your life does matter and eliminate those moments of self-doubt.

When most people think about living a Life That Matters, they think of serving others or radically serving God (Levels 2 and 3). And yes, in my opinion, those who are operating at Levels 2 and 3 are truly making it matter! But first, we need to make our lives matter so we have the energy to serve others and, potentially, a higher being.

We often get so caught up in focusing on these two levels—others and God—that we forget about ourselves, constantly sacrificing what matters to us for the sake of others. When we lose sight of ourselves and live solely for others, we risk becoming just a shell of who we truly are.

We all have responsibilities and concerns, but your number one responsibility should be you. If you don't take care of yourself, how can you take care of others? This is the advice given to caregivers so they don't burnout, to parents traveling with children on an airplane (put your mask on first before assisting others), and to parents striving for a healthy family dynamic (put the marriage first, the kids second). Put yourself numero uno to ensure you have the energy, love, and bandwidth to care for those who matter most to you.

This book is about your purpose—why you are here and what you were made to do. When you live fully, I believe you can serve those in your life even better, especially your family and God.

In the previous model, you are at the core. The core supports the outer circles, and it best supports those closest to the core. The core has to be strong, healthy, and full of energy. It can only give so much. So the further out you want to go, the more people you want to support and help, the more important it is for you to be fulfilled. Making your life matter fills you up so you can fill others up.

This book is for you. How do you make *your* life matter? This book is not about how to make those in your life matter more. That will come, and let it come—later. For now, I want to talk about you. I want you to think about you. I want you to be radically selfish, and just dream about you. Envision a beautiful, impactful life—a life so rich and fulfilled, doing the things you love, expressing yourself fully without concern, doing the things you've always wanted to do. And trust that when you do that, you'll have more impact, time, and resources to be what you need to be for those in your life. A very healthy, purpose-driven you that is living a Life That Matters.

As you learn about the concepts and components of the Life That Matters and begin to craft your Manifesto, I believe you will see an exciting life begin to unfold before your very eyes. And how exciting, because it is your life that you're making matter!

Section Summary

Are you ready to get started? Before we dive in, take a moment to give yourself some grace. You might feel more like Bob than Mark, or perhaps you're somewhere in between. Wherever you are, that's perfectly okay. This book is designed to guide you through small, achievable steps toward creating and living a Life That Matters. I encourage you to trust the process and stay curious. Remember, a Life That Matters isn't an all-or-nothing solution. You can take what resonates with you and incorporate as much or as little into your life as you choose.

If you're more like Bob, for instance, you could start by deciding that, as a person, you matter, and since you matter, you're going to start taking better care of yourself. So, you make a plan to work out and watch what you eat and drink. Seems like that would be a prudent plan, and jumping into the deep end of purpose and vision may be daunting at this time.

If you're more like Mark, you still have work to do. I encourage you to use the tools and concepts in this book to document what matters in your life and review your Life That Matters Manifesto throughout the year. Even when we know what matters, we still need to remind ourselves frequently of those things—challenge them even—or we find ourselves off course sooner than we'd think.

To live a Life That Matters, we all have to start somewhere. And since somewhere is where we currently are, why not go ahead and start there?

Here's to you creating and living an exquisite Life That Matters.

Obstacles to Mattering

2

Life Flies

If time flies, what are you doing to savor it?

There's a saying for parents of young children: "The days are long, but the months are short." I started experiencing this, and even more so did my wife, when we added child #3 to our family, and then #4. We "suddenly" found ourselves with four kids aged 8 and under (yes, I do realize what was causing that).

We love our kiddos, but man, the days were long. It was about a decade of long days, but my, how those months flew! One day it would seem like one of our kids just started walking, and then all of a sudden, he's driving? Or my little girl, who used to give me unlimited, sloppy, wet kisses, has grown up and is too embarrassed to give her dad a peck on the cheek? There were many a night when my wife and I would literally fall into bed, worn out by the daily challenges of having a brood of toddlers.

Now our toddlers are teenagers (at the time of writing this book, we have the privilege of having four teenagers all at the same time). Different challenges, but the days are still long, and it seems the months are going by even faster now.

It's not only time that flies, but life flies. And if you're not careful, it might literally fly right by you.

During this time, I discovered the following chart from Tim Urban's site, waitbutwhy.com. The chart beautifully and visually helps people see their life in months.

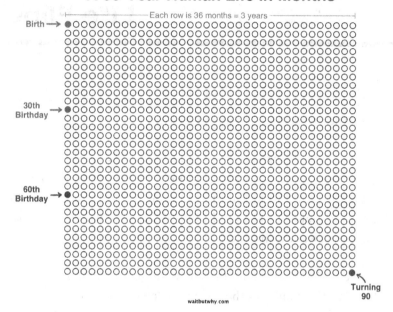

A 90-Year Human Life in Months

waitbutwhy.com

At the time, I'm 40 years old, running a digital marketing agency that is selling diamonds for a Midwestern regional jewelry retailer and multi-million dollar second, third, and fourth homes for a retirement community in South Carolina.

When I stumbled across Tim's chart and I realized that if I worked for another 20 years, that would only be 240 months and then I would be done with work. You may think that sounds like a lot. But remember, at that time my children were ages twelve to five. Days were long, but weeks were going by like days, and months were going by like weeks! 240 months, at that stage in my life, was not a very long time (spoiler alert, as we get older, time doesn't seem to slow down, it seems to speed up).

8

I didn't want to reach the end of my career and feel that I had simply sold diamonds or million-dollar houses. Not that there's anything wrong with either; I believe someone out there can live a meaningful life while selling those things. But that wasn't the case for me. So, I did some soul-searching. When I reviewed my client list, I realized we were also helping colleges and universities attract the right students—students whom these institutions could effectively educate. Through our branding services, we were enabling our clients to become better versions of themselves, and in turn, our clients were helping their students do the same. Huh.

I had an idea and brought it to my team: "What if we only worked with organizations that impact people's lives?" Given that our agency was almost entirely made up of millennials, you can imagine it wasn't a tough sell—and it wasn't.

We rebranded as Up&Up, a name reflecting our desire to uplift brands that uplift others. Ultimately, we decided to focus entirely on the higher education industry. Our work helps universities refine their brand, gain clarity about their values and what they stand for, and then market themselves authentically to attract more of the right students. We call it a win to the 5th—they (1) attract better-fit students, (2) who stay in school (avoiding the pitfalls of dropping out with debt and no degree), (3) which fosters a stronger campus culture, (4) and results in more engaged alumni, (5) who are then more likely to give back. We see that as a win for everyone involved. We call that a win for all.

When I put time in perspective—when I recognized that life flies and I didn't have forever, I realized that what I do today matters. So, I made decisions to change my actions and my path to make my life matter even more.

Start with the End In Mind: Time Binding

Mr. Campenello was my 11th-grade psychology teacher. He was a peculiar man, with his hair representative of that of bozo the clown. He was also the one teacher that taught me the only significant thing I can remember from high school: time-binding.

What is time-binding you ask? Great question. According to Mr. Campanello, time-binding is the ability to suspend your current point in time, and imagine yourself at some time in the future. An example of time-binding is delayed gratification. For instance, I choose not to eat that second piece of cake, because in a week I want to weigh less, not more. When you are able to make decisions *in the now* based on what, who, or where you want to be in the future, you're able to make better decisions. You are, after all, a sum of your choices.

Time binding enables us to make decisions about how we act and behave now, allowing us to create and eventually live out that envisioned future.

For instance:

> One attends school because he wants better opportunities in the future.

> One works out because she wants to be or stay physically fit.

> One saves money because they see themselves retiring to the beach one day.

Time binding. We act now, sometimes at some cost (but not always), because we envision a better future. It helps us make decisions, shape behavior, and invest our resources like our time, our money, and our talents to bear fruit in the future.

It's time to start time-binding. Thank you Mr. Campebello.

Start with...Your Future...In Mind

When you create a plan, starting with your future self in mind is a great principle to plan by. The same is true for living a Life That Matters. What type of life do you want to live? How do you want to be remembered? What do you want your contribution to the world to be?

One way to help you get clarity around this is to envision and write about your future self. There is an exercise in the online resources of this book (see the end of the chapter for more information), but I wanted to introduce the concept to just get you thinking for the time being. Here's my future self statement:

> *Adam lived a life of purpose. You could always find him working with men who wanted to live a life of purpose. He loved and helped those who wanted to live life to the fullest. His biggest impact was the founding of the Life That Matters Institute, which helped thousands of men around the world discover and courageously live their purpose in life. The world thanks Adam Landrum for his contribution to the movement of purpose-driven living and how he impacted 1,000's of men during his lifetime and beyond.*

Time-binding. If you don't take the time now to get a clear picture of what the end looks like, your ability to project yourself into the future as life happens gets choked out by the forces of the world. When you can't or don't time-bind, getting any traction around a Life That Matters is nearly impossible.

Start with your future self. Get a clear vision of what a Life That Matters looks like to you. For me, I want people to stand up and say,

"Adam Landrum changed my life. He challenged me to not live the status quo, but instead, to come alive, discover, and courageously live my purpose. I am grateful for that man, because I am alive and I am making a difference because of him."

That brings tears to my eyes when I write that. That is what I want. And I have so much work to do; I still have much in my life to adjust to align to that vision.

Mediocrity of the Status Quo

What if I told you that the greatest enemy to living a Life That Matters isn't existential crisis, but rather something much more subtle?

The greatest threat is a set of unwritten rules and expectations that we all agree to without a second thought: the status quo. It is the comforting blanket of mediocrity that keeps us warm at night, telling us that everything is fine just the way it is. It whispers in our ears that change is unnecessary, that striving for more is risky, and that it's better to fit in than to stand out. But here's the truth: the status quo is a thief. It steals your dreams, your passions, and your potential, all while convincing you that it's doing you a favor.

If you want to live a Life That Matters, you must first wake up to the reality that the status quo is not your friend. It's a subtle, insidious force that would rather see you numb and complacent than alive and fulfilled. To escape its grip, you need to question everything— every habit, every belief, every norm—because the moment you stop questioning is the moment you hand over the keys to your life.

The status quo is akin to somebody thinking it would be a good idea if we all did the same stupid stuff, then we couldn't blame the other guy for being stupid, and if we can't blame him, then he can't blame us.

The status quo is an unspoken social contract that says, let's keep everything mediocre. And even if the status quo doesn't make sense or it doesn't have our best interest in mind, let's just recognize it's probably providing another benefit no one is willing to name. In other words, we wouldn't do the status quo if we weren't getting something out of it.

As a far out example, imagine you've never run into the status quo. Imagine you're a foreigner, moving to this country, and you are invited to participate fully in what everyone else is doing. Here's what the pitch might look like for some of our more popular status quo offerings:

> *Can I interest you in 8 hours of screen time a day? Yes, it will be a total distraction, so you don't have to think about how much your life sucks! It'll be great. We'll fill those screens with highly opinionated and curated "news" items that piss you off, confirm your biases, and drive people you love away from you. And oh, we'll also*

pump social media through those screens so you can see all the fake, wonderful lives your friends are experiencing without you! That will in turn create a tremendous amount of anxiety, as you'll feel very insignificant. But don't worry! We'll give you a pill for that, which sure, will numb you out to some good stuff as well, but it's better not to worry about stuff, right? Now, you may deal with some depression, but so is everyone else! It's just part of life.

But to help with depression, we can offer some things that will comfort you! We know you enjoy rich food, and fast! So we're going to provide fast food and fast-casual restaurants EVERYWHERE. Eat and drink until your heart's content. Yes, we understand it will probably cause you to gain weight because great-tasting food rarely is on the healthy side. But don't worry! Everyone else will be overweight too!

Now let's talk about getting you even more comfort from just eating: drinking! You'll have access to beer and wine everywhere! They're both soooooooooo good! We'll have a bunch of breweries where you can take your kids and your dogs so they can run around! Yes, I know it's a bar, and kids, pets, and bars usually don't go together, but we'll make these breweries fun, with outdoor activities and other entertainment. And guess what (if you haven't caught on yet) — even though kids at a bar isn't the best idea, everyone's doing it so nobody cares! And hey, being a parent of little kids is hard! You can now use the beer and wine to numb yourself out and feel good in the process while your children frolic amongst the other parents grabbing a beer in the middle of the day and week!

And so goes the pitch—sorry, that's a little snarky, isn't it?

As the saying goes, "...in moderation," none of these things, if enjoyed in moderation, are bad. But when society says it's now the norm to comfort yourself ALL THE TIME, through screens, food, alcohol, and medication, we're basically just consuming and then numbing ourselves to life. And when you're numbed-out to life it's pretty tough, if not impossible, to live a Life That Matters.

Know How You Participate in the Status Quo

I think it's time we name how we participate in the status quo. We should know what it's comprised of: The things we do or accept in our lives without even thinking about it. Once we know what our participation in the status quo is, we can then decide consciously if we should or should not do that said thing.

Here are some items I consider the status quo (things we feel entitled to, won't or don't challenge, resist changing, deem acceptable regardless of actual impact):

- Binge Watching Netflix (tell me why it's a good idea to routinely watch 4-5 hours straight of television?)
- Screentime, on average, 8.3 hours per *day*[1]
- Allowing ourselves to be obese
- Allowing children to have cell phones
- Alcohol daily, and not in small amounts
- 40+ Hour Work Week (does it have to be 40 hours?)
- 5 Day Work Week (does it have to be 5 days?)
- Retirement (is it a good idea to retire?)

---

[1] **Nielsen.** *The Nielsen Total Audience Report: April 2020.* Nielsen, April 2020, https://www.nielsen.com/insights/2020/the-nielsen-total-audience-report-april-2020/. In-text citation: (Nielsen, 2020)

- Father's spending only one hour a day with their children[2]
- Travel Sports for the kids (the family sacrifice of time and money spent on most kids who won't make it to the next level)
- Divorce (Over 50%)[3]
- Living together before married (those that do are more likely to get divorced)[4]
- And, on and on.

I'm starting to sound like my grandmother, "This country is going to hell in a handbasket!" But unfortunately, the list above is *normal*. We simply do these things without really thinking about them. Why? Because it's the status quo and the status quo gives you permission to participate without asking anyone else or yourself if that's a good idea.

Let's stop and think about some of these things for just a second (i.e.time-bind). Should we invest tens of thousands of dollars for Johnny's baseball? Should we devote every weekend of our summer to travel to play baseball? Split our family up, take turns going to God-knows-what-city for this weekend? Is that a good idea?

I don't know. It might be. And if you consciously think it through and decide as parents, then yes, travel baseball might be a good thing for Johnny and the family.

But many people don't even think about it. The decision really looks something like this: All of Johnny's friends are doing travel baseball,

---

[2] **Pew Research Center.** "Key Facts About Dads in the U.S." *Pew Research Center*, 15 June 2023, https://www.pewresearch.org/short-reads/2023/06/15/key-facts-about-dads-in-the-us/#:~:text=Most%20of%20dads'%20time%20with,regardless%20of%20the%20children's%20ages.

[3] **Forbes Advisor.** "Divorce Statistics and Facts in 2023." *Forbes*, 18 Sept. 2023, https://www.forbes.com/advisor/legal/divorce/divorce-statistics/.

[4] Manning, Wendy D., Pamela J. Smock and Arielle Kuperberg.(2021). "Cohabitation and Marital Dissolution: A Comment on Rosenfield and Roseler (2019)." Journal of Marriage and Family, 83, 260-267. doi: 10.1111/jomf.12724

his friends' parents have signed up for the madness, so I guess we're doing it too! That's the status quo. That's what it does. It takes our brain away and we just follow the crowd like zombie sheep.

What status quo things do you unconsciously partake in that may interfere with your desire to live a Life That Matters? Where should you change your beliefs or activities so you are better positioned to live a Life That Matters?

Why am I so fired up about the status quo? Because the status quo does not want you to live a Life That Matters. So in order to live a Life That Matters, you will have to examine how and if your life is influenced by the status quo, and challenge those assumptions to live differently.

4

Don't Fear Fear Itself

In light of the tremendous pressure to conform and abide by the status quo, it never ceases to amaze me how awesome and unique people are. I'm always blown away by the talent, intelligence, abilities, and personalities people have. It's like people are superheroes, with their own unique combination of strengths and characteristics.

You are a superhero at some level. You have your own unique strengths, but you have your unique weaknesses, too, your own personal kryptonite. And there's one huge weakness you have that brings all of us to our knees.

The Mother of All Kryptonite

Our commonly-shared Kryptonite isn't in a lead box. It's not from another world. It's not a weapon someone else wields. No, our kryptonite doesn't come from outside of us. It comes from within.

Our greatest weakness is but a whisper. It whispers many things, but ultimately with one core message. The whisper condescends, chides, reminds, told-you-so's, doubts, shakes its head, and is constantly saying:

- You're not that good
- Who do you think you are?
- You're not fast enough
- Or smart enough
- Or strong enough

Ultimately, it all boils down to one core message:

- *YOU AREN'T ENOUGH*

I'm here to tell you that that's a bunch of crap. You are Enough. You are more than Enough. But there's one in us, who's job is to have us doubt ourselves, and live in constant fear that the next failure is right around the corner.

In life coaching we call this guy your gremlin. You have several of these guys. One of my gremlins I've named Alvin. He's the one who reminds me that I'm all alone—that I must navigate this thing called life on my own, that I can't trust anyone, that people are out to hurt me, and that to survive, it's better if I'm by myself.

Isn't that lovely? He is lovely actually, as I've grown to love him instead of hating him. It's quite natural to hate your gremlins. They usually give us some very hard messages to hear. But instead of hating him,

I've decided to love him. If I'm oblivious to him, I don't have the choice to love him. I'm also not even aware he's trying to give me a message. I just have this feeling of fear, distrust, and a constant looking over my shoulder. But now that I've gotten to know Alvin, I've given him a different job. I've asked him to keep me informed when he senses something is off, especially when it's wise to protect myself or others. I've asked him to deemphasize this alone thing, because although that's a fear, it's probably not a reality, so I can free myself up from that worry.

In coaching, the gremlins are deep, held beliefs that are often unconscious. Because of that, we are committed to believing their message without even realizing it.

Alvin's whispering is just another message of: "You're not enough." Why will I be taken advantage of? Because I'm not enough. Why will someone hurt me? Because I wasn't strong or smart enough [to protect myself]. Why will I end up alone? Because I'm not enough [to be loved by someone].

And guess what happens when you're not enough? You stop trying. You don't believe in yourself. Your self-confidence is shot. You sit down to write a book and your gremlins start going crazy: You've never written a book before! Who do you think you are? You don't know enough! You can't do this. What a waste of time. People are going to think it's garbage. It won't make a difference!

And so I smile. I open my arms to my gremlins and invite them to join me. I tell them, thank you for that message. How do you think I could be successful? What would enough look like? What do you think I should do?

You see, they're just scared. They're just scared, and they want to be assured everything is okay. Their very existence depends on me needing them. If I don't need them, if they can't worry me, then they do not need to exist. And so I turn them into watchmen and consultants. And when I hear "Not Enough" coming from my inner critics, I engage them. I move towards them, and ask them, what is it that I need to learn? What gift could they give me? Because I do believe that they have useful information. It just needs to be coaxed from them.

Don't Run

The mistake people make is they try to run from their gremlins. Or ignore them. They try to stuff them down. It doesn't work. Your gremlins are part of you. They've been around for a long while, and they aren't going anywhere.

Don't run from them, embrace them. Run to them. Respect them. Listen to them. Give them some time. Correct them by politely saying, "No, Alvin, I am enough. But thank you for wanting to protect me."

If you are aware of your gremlins and you love them instead of ignoring them or fighting them, they can help you make your life matter instead of keeping you from making it matter.

Section Summary

The three biggest obstacles to living a Life That Matters is a:

1. Lack of a sense of urgency, thinking you have all the time in the world
2. Unconscious adoption of the status quo, and
3. General fear that you have around failure and not being enough.

If we can realize that:

- **Time is flying.** Life is both short and fast, so mattering needs to start *now*, not tomorrow.

- **The Status Quo is optional.** If it doesn't matter, don't do it. Just because it's the status quo and permissible doesn't mean you should do it. If socially accepted behavior doesn't align with your values, the amount of time you have available in a day, or simply just isn't something that serves you, then consciously choose not to participate!

- **Fear is normal.** You are enough and know that you are not alone in thinking that you aren't. Everyone deals with this fear in one shape or another. Simply believing you are enough and reminding yourself that you are enough is a good habit to have for the rest of your life.

SECTION 2

The Proactive Life

In my early 20's, I read a book by Hyrum Smith called *The 10 Natural Laws of Time and Life Management*. In that book he introduced the concept of proactive living. As an early 20 something, I had this innate desire to matter. I knew that I wasn't put on this earth simply to eat, work, and sleep. I was full of energy, ideas, and abilities. How could I put it to use to matter? Hyrum's concept of the Proactive Life was exactly what I was looking for.

The concept is quite simple and it makes a whole lot of sense. Here's the idea: most people live a reactionary life. They wait for things to happen and then respond. Hyrum was presenting a different concept. What if instead, we lived *proactively*? We determined what was important to us, made a plan, committed to that plan, and *lived* that plan?

Brilliant. But the key here is to actually *live*. Easier said than done.

The problem with human nature is it's built to react. We are hard-wired, reactionary professionals. And that comes from our default operating system that is run by our Ego. And the Ego's sole objective is to protect and survive. And to survive, we must be really good at *reacting*.

To better understand our survival system, we need to understand its origination. Survival systems of course are hard wired into all animals, including man. So picture this: the caveman steps out of his cave, and watch out!, a sabertooth tiger lunges from above, going for his head. Caveman ducks, swoops up his club and whacks the tiger over the head before he becomes Mr. Tiger's lunch (and that's how sabretooths went extinct. Joking.).

Survival is about reacting. Living in the now, in the moment, and living for day-to-day sustenance. In today's world, we may have difficulty grasping this survival concept. Do we need this anymore?

Recently, my son and I visited Africa for the first time. It was a pseudo-mission trip aimed at learning more about an organization we were interested in getting involved with and supporting. As a foreigner in their land, the one thing that struck me was how much the natives were living for just today. Not out of a woke-state mind you, but out of necessity. Every day, they had to go make today's living, get today's water, and today's food. Shelter wasn't even a given. Half-built buildings are everywhere because they don't have access to financing. They're waiting to earn enough money so they can buy the next round of bricks. It takes the average African years to build a simple structure.

This stark reality underscores a fundamental aspect of human existence: the operating system is built to survive, to identify threats, and respond to survive. In a first world country, we are not too concerned about opening the front door and being taken down by a tiger. Instead, our Ego is constantly scanning the horizon for other threats. Am I going to get fired for being late? Was that comment by my spouse intentionally meant to harm me? Is my neighbor building on my property? And so on.

We're wired to react, therefore, the idea of living proactively is not natural. Proactive Living by its very nature requires forethought, planning, discipline, and execution. Since our default mode is to react, we simply recognize this in order to build habits that rewire our reactive operating system into a proactive operating system.

The Proactive Life

Living a proactive life is living the life you want to live, intentionally. That means:

1. You **know** the life that you want to live, and
2. You **commit** to live such a life, and
3. You **plan** that life, and

4. You are **disciplined** and start working the plan, living your life.

So where do you start—how do you know what life it is you want to live? You probably have a good idea already and of course you're living the life you want at some level. But could it be more? Could your life matter more? Could it be bigger?

If I were a betting man, I'd bet you haven't allowed yourself to dream as big as you could, meaning, the life that you have in mind is smaller than it could be. And that's normal (remember our gremlins keep us from dreaming too big). In the how-to section and on our companion website, you will be introduced to some exercises to help you expand your dreams.

The Life That Matters Manifesto is all about knowing and committing to the life you want to live. Let's dive into understanding what components make up the Manifesto.

5

The Life That Matters Components and Hierarchy

There's a hierarchy of components that make up a Life That Matters. They are not necessarily building blocks, and they do not need to be done linearly. For instance, you can believe in a higher power but not understand your purpose. However, if you are able to articulate each of these components, commit to them, and live a life of integrity that is true to them, you will be maximizing your life to matter.

On the left side of the model, you see the sequence "Know → Commit → Alive → Faith." A person living a Life That Matters is one who has made the decision to truly become alive. In contrast, a life that is not alive belongs to someone who merely exists, living reactively rather than proactively.

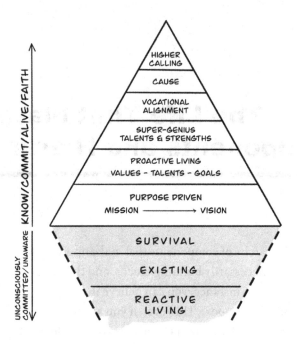

A person's life that is alive, has character. He has values. He lives a passionate life, with hobbies, preferences, and desires. He loves to compete or to paint or to read or to cook—or all of the above! A person with a life alive has dreams and goals and aspirations! His life is in motion and someone you want to be around.

A Life That Matters is alive, and that life requires commitment to stay alive. The person's Life That Matters begins to understand his purpose, and he begins to shape a vision and starts living proactively, on a mission. A person whose life matters commits to understanding his Super-Genius, identifying his talents and strengths and commits to use them for the greater good—and for his good.

As he moves further up the hierarchy, he begins to believe in something bigger than himself—the ultimate goal of a Life That Matters. He believes in a cause that he hopes to influence and contribute to, aspiring to see it come to fruition not only through his own efforts but also through the contributions of countless other purpose-driven individuals.

And his faith blossoms more—trusting in the unseen—as he puts his life into the hands of his God, trusting and depending on an unseen God to guide him through life, to sustain him, protect him, love him, and provide for him. In return, he will love his God, serve him and be obedient to him. He will share the love of his God with others, loving others as he does himself. And all of that requires a tremendous amount of faith, yet a simple faith as we are told, like the faith of a child.

Dream Big, Start Small

As I previously mentioned, the Life That Matters isn't sequential. I don't want you to be intimidated by all the stuff you will need to do. Just start small. Start at the bottom, with your purpose. If you already know your purpose, then move onto your values, then identify your passions, and so on. As you build your Life That Matters Manifesto, you will choose what components to include and what to exclude.

So are you ready? Are you ready to start building the components to a Life That Matters? We'll break down each component, starting from the bottom up.

You may have varying levels of familiarity with these components. Some you might already know well, making them just a review for you. Others, like your values, you may inherently understand but have never explicitly written down or articulated. Still, some components may be entirely new territory for you.

Wherever you are in the process, you're building your Life That Matters Manifesto. By the time you finish this book, you'll have the opportunity to have identified all of your components that make up the Life That Matters Manifesto.

SECTION 3

The Life That Matters Manifesto

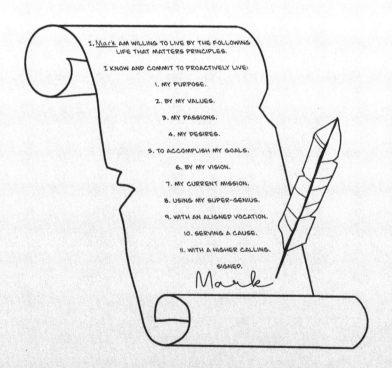

I, _Mark_ AM WILLING TO LIVE BY THE FOLLOWING
LIFE THAT MATTERS PRINCIPLES.

I KNOW AND COMMIT TO PROACTIVELY LIVE:

1. MY PURPOSE.

2. BY MY VALUES.

3. MY PASSIONS.

4. MY DESIRES.

5. TO ACCOMPLISH MY GOALS.

6. BY MY VISION.

7. MY CURRENT MISSION.

8. USING MY SUPER-GENIUS.

9. WITH AN ALIGNED VOCATION.

10. SERVING A CAUSE.

11. WITH A HIGHER CALLING.

SIGNED,

Mark

A manifesto serves as a powerful public declaration, and in this case, it's about something deeply personal—your life! The first objective is for you to understand what each component means to you, so that you know what A Life That Matters signifies for you personally. Whether you choose to share your Life That Matters Manifesto with others is entirely up to you; however, once it's complete, I encourage you to do so. I've found that when I share things like my vision or current mission, relevant opportunities often seem to appear unexpectedly. So, yes, I encourage you to share your Manifesto once it's finished. A Life That Matters is meant to be shared and lived with others.

The rest of the book will go over the eleven Principles of The Life That Matters. The goal is to introduce these concepts to you and for you to be familiar with them, but I didn't want to stop there. I wanted to provide you the necessary resources so you can do the work yourself and create your own Manifesto. Visit us online at www.madetomatter. coach/manifesto for those resources once you're done reading the book.

My Life That Matters Manifesto

I, [name], am willing to live by the following Life That Matters Principles.

I know and commit to proactively live:

1. My purpose.
    I will live a purpose-driven life, knowing I am here for a reason and who I am matters and what I do matters.

2. By my values.
    I will make choices both big and small based on my values. My actions will match my beliefs, regardless of the cost.

3. My passions.

   I will honor my passions, those interests, talents, hobbies, and pleasures that fill me up and give me energy; that make me come alive.

4. My Desires.

   I will know my lifetime desires, the ideals that I want to realize and which I want to be known for when I am gone.

5. To Accomplish My Goals.

   I will write my goals down and always be working to achieve them. I will revisit my goals regularly and update them so they are always relevant.

6. By My Vision.
   I will know where I am going and where I want to arrive. I can see that destination clearly in my mind, and I share and invite others to join me.

7. My Current Mission.
   I will always be on a mission, accomplishing the next milestone in life on my way to realize my vision.

8. Using My Super-Genius.
   I will use my Super-Genius as much as possible to maximize my impact for myself and others.

9. With an Aligned Vocation.
   I will have an occupation that allows me to use my Super-Genius and is aligned with the other components of my Life That Matters Manifesto.

10. Serving a Cause.
    I will serve something larger than me, choosing to serve a cause or movement that I am passionate about.

11. With a Higher Calling.
    I will seek out my higher calling and orient my life to that calling to accomplish the God-given mission I am given.

[Signature]

[Date]

Manifesto #1:
Live Your Purpose

I will live a purpose-driven life, knowing I am here for a reason and who I am matters and what I do matters.

Purpose, purpose, purpose. Everyone wants me to live my purpose.

Well, yeah. It's the reason you exist, so don't you think you should live it? Maybe figure it out at least? And then decide what to do with it? Or we can continue to ignore it and just get busy with life. How about we just keep ourselves distracted and be miserable? I joke—sort of.

What does it take for you to figure out your purpose? For some reason, figuring out your purpose is like trying to conceptualize eternity. I remember doing that when I was six years old, and it hurt my brain—a lot.

I've done the brain-hurting thing with purpose as well, but it doesn't have to be that way. In my mid-twenties, I wrote my purpose statement. Since then, I've read books on purpose, I've been coached on purpose, I've taken courses on purpose, assessments on purpose, and written and given speeches on the subject of purpose.

And guess what? The purpose statement I wrote over 20 years ago perfectly captured the essence of what I would still say my purpose is today.

Years ago, I was on a walk with my wife, and I shared with her this new revelation I had regarding my purpose. She stopped in her tracks, looked at me, and said, "You've been telling this to me for 20 years. Stop thinking about it and start doing it!"

She actually didn't say that last part, but she should have. No matter how often I try to refine my purpose, I keep coming back to the same old purpose over and over again. It's in my blood. There's no shaking it. My purpose is right there, patiently waiting to be rediscovered—yet again—but really waiting for me to do something with it.

My point is this: You know your purpose. Loved ones in your life probably know your purpose better than you do. This doesn't have to be difficult, and it doesn't have to be hard. You shouldn't have to shed blood, sweat, or tears to define your purpose.

You should—and could—probably just blurt your purpose statement out right now, and it would be close enough. Let's do it. Blurt out your purpose. Say the following out loud:

My name is [My Name] and my purpose is to _____.

How'd that go? Okay, maybe not great. But let's explore some concepts of purpose so at the end of this chapter, you can complete that sentence with some level of confidence.

Your Purpose is What You're Naturally Attracted To

You've been living your purpose all this time. Think about the moments that have given you some of the greatest satisfaction in life. While you were doing those fulfilling activities, you were probably also using your gifts—your Super-Genius (more on that in a later chapter).

For example, here's what I love to do: Give me a group of people who are curious, who want to build self-awareness, and who are willing to be challenged. Put us in an environment that offers a rich experience full of great food, learning, and adventure, and you'll find one guy who is in his element—me. Yeah, my purpose is to coach leaders and entrepreneurs—to challenge them to stop living the status quo and instead courageously discover and live their purpose. I get goosebumps just thinking about that.

My personality (another key to purpose) thrives on intimacy and depth. I have a desire to go deep and talk about things you've never discussed with anyone else. Let's drag all of that crap out and deal with it. Then let's move on and go kick ass and take names. I'm your guy if you want to get after it. That's my purpose: to free people from the status quo so they can thrive by living their purpose.

There, I just did it again. See? I haven't given you my official purpose statement. Instead, I've shared stories that capture the essence of my purpose. They all point back to the same thing. And I bet you have those stories and that essence, too.

What is your essence? What are you passionate about? What fires you up? What gives you goosebumps? What makes you cry? What breaks your heart? And my favorite question: What are you so passionate about that when the subject comes up, you pound the table with your fist? Answer those questions, pull out the common essence—and therein lies your purpose.

Get Clear on the Definitions

There can be a lot of confusion around the terms "purpose," "mission," and "vision." Purpose, simply put, is why you exist. Don't confuse your current mission with your purpose. Your mission is a short-term objective that aligns with your purpose and serves as a stepping stone to your vision. A vision is a picture of an ideal future. Your vision is the North Star. It's something you may never fully reach, but it orients you and guides your direction in life. Your mission is like the North Pole; hypothetically, you can reach it. It's a destination and a goal you can actually attain. It may take several years and a lot of hard work, but you can get there.

I used to confuse purpose and mission. In Tim Kelley's book True Purpose, he explains that "a mission is a specific task that needs to be performed."[5] In my experience, a mission is a short-term objective (typically 1–5 years) that represents your purpose in your current life stage. In other words, it's the specific initiative that needs to get done to further your vision while staying true to your purpose. Your mission may change based on what's currently happening in your life. For instance, when I was a newlywed without any kids, I mentored young men, sometimes having two to three mentees at any given time. However, when my wife and I started having children, and they began playing sports and attending school events, I experienced a season of life where I no longer had the discretionary time to mentor young men. My purpose and vision didn't change, but my current mission did.

Don't confuse your purpose with your mission. Your purpose is why you exist—the essence of who you are and what you're about. The essence of your purpose will not change in your lifetime, but your mission will likely change many times throughout your life.

For me, that was an exciting revelation: My purpose was foundational, and I would use that foundation to embark on many missions throughout my life, all while striving toward my vision. Purpose → Missions → Vision. How fun is that?

---

[5] Kelley, T. (2009). *True Purpose: 12 Strategies for Discovering the Difference You Are Meant to Make*. Transcendent Solutions Press.

Keep it Simple: Get the Essence

One of the best things I've done around purpose is to make a purpose assessment. Getting the essence of your purpose is more important than getting it exact. On my site, www.madetomatter. coach/manifesto – you can find and take the assessment. It takes 10 minutes and produces a super-simple deliverable: your purpose essence statement.

I've had many people take this assessment and over 90% of those feel like it nailed their purpose quite well. In my experience, my purpose-essence, "Living Purpose," again, points to my essence. I live, sleep, eat, and breathe purpose. I do. Nearly everything I do has a purpose. I can't not do purpose. My first book that I wrote, though I had ten different topics I could have written on, I chose the subject of purpose. Of course.

And please realize, I'm poking fun at myself a bit too. I'm not saying, "See how great I am! See how on purpose I am!" What I'm saying is that when your purpose is alive within you, you can't not do it (double negatives here are intentional). You might be so "on purpose" that you come across as a little overbearing. But damn, isn't that exactly what the world needs more of? As John Eldredge, author of *Wild at Heart*, paraphrased Howard Thurman, "Don't ask what the world needs. Ask yourself, 'What makes me come alive?' Because what the world needs is people who have come alive."[6]

Permission for Meltdown

Why You Shouldn't Have Just One Midlife Crisis; You should Have Several

---

[6] John Eldredge, Wild at Heart: Discovering the Secret of a Man's Soul (Nashville: Thomas Nelson, 2001), 200.

I had my first "midlife" crisis at around 25. It was a little early, so I dubbed it a quarter-life crisis. As a card-carrying member of GenX, I like to joke that I'm half Millennial. The purpose-driven, "gonna save the world" mentality is in GenX, just like it is with Millennials. So, at 25, I was working for a really big accounting firm, and I thought, "Oh my gosh, am I possibly going to audit companies' books for the rest of my life?" The answer was an absolute no. So, I quit.

And what did I do? I left sunny Southern California and moved in with my in-laws in Charleston, SC. Yep. If that wasn't enough (moving in with the in-laws will put anyone into midlife crisis mode), I joined another accounting firm. But this time, I had a brilliant idea: I wouldn't do audit; I would do tax, because doing people's taxes is so much better than auditing companies' books!

It took me one miserable busy season to realize I was done with the CPA life, and I desperately needed a change. At 25, I was married, living with my in-laws, and absolutely miserable in my career. I'd spent most of my short adult life up until that point devoted to getting an accounting degree and passing the CPA exam. And I was quitting.

I was in a quarter-life crisis.

Then the phone rang. It was my friend, mentor, and the pastor who married my wife and me. He told me he was moving to Atlanta to start a church (his first church was a smashing success in terms of how new churches go). He didn't ask me to join him necessarily; he just said, "My wife and I have been praying that you and Shely would join us in starting this." I quickly replied, "No, do not pray for that!" I had zero ambition to go into ministry.

It took me about two weeks of misery to accept his unspoken offer. After praying about it, my wife and I decided to join him in Atlanta. And to me, it was no small decision. I was taking the cloth and going full-time into ministry. There would be no looking back—that was all there was to it.

About 18 months into the church start-up, a businessman named Bill Shaw sat across from me at lunch one day and, with an implied accusation, asked, "Adam, what are you doing?" I responded in confusion, believing what I was doing was damn noble, "I'm in the ministry." He then said, "You weren't made to be in the ministry. You were made to be a businessman." And just like that, it struck a nerve. I knew he was right, and I knew it was time to act.

I had confused "vocation as a purpose" with the idea that purpose drives vocation. I believed that if I were to live out my purpose, then my job would have to be the main expression of that purpose. But purpose isn't the only factor to consider when trying to optimize a job. Your talents, passions, and interests, to name a few, should also play a role (more on that in the Manifesto #9 section). I realized I could still own a business and "do ministry," which I loved and was passionate about. A year later, I started my agency, Up&Up.

It was abundantly clear that accounting was the wrong profession for me, as it had very little to do with my purpose, and the church lacked my passion for business. But I had invested so much in that career at the time, I needed something major to break me free of that career path. That change agent appeared as a quarter-life crisis and a timely prophecy from a mentor to get me on the right course.

Get the Message Early

A midlife crisis screams: something needs to change! It's like a man wakes up one day and asks himself, *How did I get here?* Balding, overweight, out of shape, in a dead-end job, finances in shambles, married to someone he doesn't know anymore, with a brood of ungrateful kids... Yeah, that might be a good reason to flip out.

But we wait too long, right? Instead of taking inventory along the way, we save it all for one grand finale and decide we're going to go out in a big ball of flames. We get divorced, buy a sports car, date someone 15 years younger, and just look plain silly.

Let's do the midlife crisis right. Let's take sabbaticals. Extended vacations. Truly unplug. Read some good books. Do some soul searching by building time into our lives for reflection. Take inventory. Have honest, tough conversations with our loved ones. And ultimately, be courageous enough to act and change, even if it means taking a step backward to get started.

For instance, I'm on a sabbatical now as I write this book. Do I feel a midlife crisis coming on? A little bit. Not one that I think will bring me down in flames, but one where I might make some decisions that could change aspects of my life. And what I'm saying is—that's OK. That's good. We should take time to evaluate and consider making a game change before it's too late...or before we die, having lived a miserable life.

Bob Buford wrote a great book called *Halftime*.[7] It's for those who have been successful in the first half of their life, and now want the second half to have significance and meaning. You want to make your life matter. In other words, *Halftime* uncovers the midlife existential question, which is quite natural and normal. Don't resist it. Lean into it. Embrace it. Be open to hearing the message. Your life isn't perfect. You don't have it all figured out. That's okay, and it's okay to change!

Give yourself permission to have a midlife crisis. I know it's hard, but maybe it's time to second-guess your career and do something completely different. Maybe it's time to stop drinking. Change your friend group. Hire a chef and a personal trainer and say *enough is*

---

[7] Buford, B. (1994). *Halftime: Moving from success to significance.* William Morrow and Company.

enough. Tell people you're struggling and that you think you're in a midlife crisis. Get support.

As the saying goes, "A crisis is a terrible thing to waste." Most of us will deal with a midlife crisis. If you do, make it count. Make it a good one, and don't be the guy with so much pent-up angst that he ends up going off the deep end because he didn't break up that big midlife crisis into smaller, manageable ones.

I'll leave you with this analogy: A guided missile hits its target 99.9% of the time. It's fascinating how it accomplishes that. The operator programs the flight path, and once launched, the missile follows that path. But as you can imagine, many variables affect it—atmosphere, weather, wind, changes in temperature, and even a rotating Earth. So, what does the missile's guidance system do? It makes countless small adjustments along the way—course corrections. When we say "corrections," we acknowledge that something was off or needed to change. So one could say the missile got off the right path. So be it. The corrections are made, and now it's back on target! The missile adjusts its path in mid-flight. Like a guided missile, when you know why you exist (your purpose), have a path (vision), know your target (mission), and continually course-correct (make adjustments, i.e., "midlife" crisis) with your purpose, vision, and mission in mind, you hit your target! Every. Time.

Now that should make you cry. Go and have your midlife crises. Just make your corrections small and frequent, and you'll stay on course.

Summary

- **You know your purpose.** Keep it simple. Answer the questions in the how-to section, take the purpose assessment found in the same section.

- **Your Purpose Doesn't Change**, but your Missions do. Missions are short-term (1-5 year) initiatives that are supported by your purpose and aligned to your vision.
- **Have a Mid-life Crisis**. Actually, have several. Try not to wait to have a big one. Instead, have a bunch of small ones and make the necessary adjustments along the way to get aligned with your purpose.

###

To develop your Manifesto #1, visit the how-to section in the book and online at www.madetomatter.coach/manifesto.

Manifesto #2:
Live Your Values

I will make choices both big and small based on my values. My actions will match my beliefs, regardless of the cost.

We often think we know what we value, but do we really? Values aren't just what we say they are; they are what we live out every single day. The gap between what we claim to prioritize and what we actually do is where our true values lie.

For instance, we can say we value family, but if we don't spend time with them, then we really don't value them, do we? We can say we value our marriage, but if we refuse to invest the time and money to keep it healthy, then we really don't value that marriage.

Our actions, calendar, and checkbook reveal what we truly value. What you have in your life is not only a reflection of the choices you've made but also a more accurate representation of what you value.

I was interviewing a candidate for a new role at my company. She told me she was excited to work for a purpose-driven company. She loved that we focused on people and found it refreshing compared to companies that only focus on making money (how evil!). I asked her, since she valued purpose, what her purpose was. She looked at me blankly. She couldn't answer. Eventually, she fumbled out something about serving her husband. I let that slide because, honestly, most people don't know their purpose, right? So, I pressed on the other thing she said she loved—the idea of helping people. I asked how she helped others. "Oh, well...I don't currently do that. I just don't have the time," she responded.

Uh-huh. In other words, she said she valued purpose but didn't have one, and she valued helping others, but she didn't make time to do that either. No problem. I'm not judging her—other than judging that I didn't believe she valued what she said she valued. Her actions didn't match her words; as they say, she wasn't walking the talk.

Once you know what you value, it will shape your decisions, choices, and actions. For instance, your values can guide you in choosing the type of company you want to work for, how and where you spend your time, who you invest in, and which friendships or relationships you should keep—or move on from. You already value what you value, so this is not about creating your values as much as it is about discovering them. Once you've uncovered what you truly value, you can begin to clarify and articulate those values—first to yourself, and then to others in your life.

When you align your actions with your values, life starts to matter.

Summary

Your values are deep within you, an invisible force that guides what you do. When your actions don't align with your beliefs, that causes major dissonance, intergrity breaches, and energy leaks. In otherwords, it's exhausting. Aligning your actions to your values gives you energy to live a Life that Matters.

1. Know your values
2. (Take the Values Assessment at www.madetomatter.coach/manifesto)

3. Share your values with others for accountability
4. Live your values

###

To develop your Manifesto #2, visit the how-to section in the book and online at www.madetomatter.coach/manifesto.

Manifesto #3:
Live Your Passions

I will honor my passions, those interests, talents, hobbies, and pleasures that fill me up and give me energy; that make me come alive.

What fills you up? What gives you energy? What can't you get enough of? Those are your passions. Living your passions is living life. It's the fuel to a Life That Matters. It's usually what's missing in our mid-life, once we wake up and realize that the passion is gone. You've heard people say it about marriage or a career. There's just no more passion left. It's not fun anymore.

Life can be messy and complicated, often pulling us in different directions. As we get caught up in it, our priorities shift, and one day we might realize that our lives have become all work and no play. We've taken on a myriad of responsibilities, and gradually, sometimes intentionally, sometimes inadvertently, we've let go of our passions. It can happen subtly—like, we used to love reading, but by the end of the day, we're too exhausted to pick up a book. Or we used to golf, but with the demands of family life, there's just no time left. Perhaps we were avid bike riders, but since our child started playing travel-ball, our weekends have gone from being filled with riding to sitting in the bleachers.

Ah, yes, the sacrifices. Sometimes you must sacrifice a passion or two. But also realize you are making choices that are sucking the life out of you, too. Do so carefully. And if you realized you have in fact done that, I encourage you to start working some of your passions back in.

Often, what fills you up as an adult is rooted in what you loved as a kid. You played games, created endlessly (remember all those drawings, paintings, and art projects in school?), danced, and sang without a care in the world. You had imaginary friends, played make-believe games, and were brimming with curiosity and creativity, full of boundless energy.

Sure, part of that energy came from simply being a kid—kids are naturally full of energy. But another reason was your unconstrained passion and curiosity. Many adults realize they've stopped doing something they loved as a child and find joy in returning to it. For example, did you ride a bike as a kid? Was it fun? Do you still ride now? In our town, there's a bike trail. You don't have to be a serious cyclist to enjoy it. My wife and I often ride to a coffee shop just three miles away. We savor a croissant, sip coffee, talk, laugh, and then ride back home, feeling the wind in our hair. I know it sounds a bit cheesy, but it fills us up—we love it. Think back to your childhood. What did you love doing? Fishing? Boating? Shooting? Playing sports? If you feel passion is lacking in your life, I encourage you to bring some of those childhood joys back into your routine.

What are some things you've done that you truly enjoyed? Are there activities you've never tried but think you might enjoy? Do you like listening to live music? If so, how often do you go in a year? What about live performances—do you enjoy those? How often do you attend, or how often would you like to? Do you enjoy traveling? Where's your favorite destination? Do you have a "happy place," like a vacation spot, a cabin, or the lake?

Summary

Passion. In the How-to section of the book, you'll build your passion list. I hope you're looking forward to it. It's time to have more fun in your life!*

###

To develop your Manifesto #3, visit the how-to section in the book and online at www.madetomatter.coach/manifesto.

*It's also very rewarding to do this for significant others. Discover what passions they want in their lives and help them pursue those. I remember as a young married couple, I wondered what my lovely wife and mother of two small children would love to do. She was pouring herself out as a wife and mom, and I could tell there wouldn't be much left if I didn't step in. We didn't have a lot of money at the time, but she loved to work out, so I got her a YMCA membership (a big recurring expense for our tight budget). In addition to working out, it gave her a 60- to 90-minute break from the kids because the YMCA had childcare. Although we couldn't "afford" it, I realized it was too important for her. She loves working out, and she needed some passion in her life, badly! I figured out how to make it happen!

Manifesto #4:
Live Your Desires

I will know my lifetime desires, the ideals that I want to realize and which I want to be known for when I am gone.

There's a difference between a desire and a goal. A desire is a defining attribute or characteristic about your life that you want to happen. A goal is something you want to achieve. Live a life "Madly in Love" is a desire. It's something to strive for and it's a great desire to have. Getting Married is a goal. It's something that is specific, measurable, and achievable. The desire, being Madly in Love, is something one will have to constantly work on. Getting married is literally an event (not to be confused with marriage) and therefore is a goal. Desires shape our goals. They are aspirational, qualitative, and serve as a north star that guides a Life That Matters.

A desire is more like an ideal. It's qualitative and more about the journey than the destination. Goals, on the other hand, are specific, measurable, and quantifiable—you know when you've accomplished a goal.

For example, one of my desires is to have deep friendships in my life. I want to live a life surrounded by and defined by friends with whom I've gone very deep. The number of friends isn't as important as the quality of the friendships. What matters is that those friendships are deep—like brotherhood deep. That's a core desire in my life.

One of my recent goals was to start a men's fraternity. I wanted to do life with guys who had similar experiences and values (business leaders who love business, learning, fun, and brotherhood).

I set the goal to start Fellows International, and by golly, that goal has been achieved. It aligns with my desire to have deep friendships.

Your desires are lifelong. Since a desire often represents an ideal, it will always be something you can strive to improve upon. At times, you may take a step back, but then you work harder to take two steps forward, continuing to make progress.

Desires like having a Great Marriage, being a Loving Father, and having Deep Friendships are lifelong pursuits. At the end of your fulfilling life, you'll look back and say that you lived a life that mattered because you knew and proactively strived to live a life that satisfied those desires, even though there was always more that could have been done.

Summary

Desires are like ideals, something to strive towards but never fully attained.

Goals are like projects, they have a start and a stop, they can be achieved and marked "done."

1. Know your Desires before you set Goals
2. Set your Goals to Align with your Desires.

To develop your Manifesto #4, visit the how-to section in the book and online at www.madetomatter.coach/manifesto.

Manifesto #5:
Live to Accomplish
Your Goals

I will write my goals down and always be working to achieve them. I will revisit my goals regularly and update them so they are always relevant.

Understanding the connection between your goals and your lifetime desires is essential for long-term fulfillment. By aligning your goals with what truly matters to you—your lifetime desires—you create a roadmap that not only guides your actions but also fuels your motivation. This approach ensures that every step you take, whether it's over a few months or several years, is moving you closer to a Life that Matters.

While we established that Desires are ideals and are meant to be strived towards, goals are specific objectives that are meant to be achieved. They should be Specific, Measurable, Attainable, Relevant, and Timely (also known as SMART Goals). Because goals are often time-bound, I typically use and recommend setting them for three years, one year, and quarterly periods. The exciting part about using these defined timeframes is that they allow you to align your goals with your deepest desires.

That's right. If your desire is to have Deep Friendships, you can set a goal for this quarter that moves you closer to that desire. Expand that to a year and three years, and suddenly, you're making serious progress toward a lifetime desire.

Starting with the end in mind—the lifetime desire—the planning might look like this:

Lifetime Desire 1 ← 3 Year Goal ← 1 Year Goal ← Quarterly Goal
Deep Friendships ← Guys Trip to Ireland ← Do Golf League ← Start Men's Group

Three years is long enough that you can dream a bit, but short enough that you need to start acting soon. A one-year goal gives you time to achieve something significant, while still creating the pressure to stay accountable. Quarterly goals should be highly achievable (make sure they are!), giving you the urgency to act now. They reset every quarter, allowing you to adjust them as needed to stay aligned with your one-year and three-year goals. All three goal periods should align with your lifetime desire to keep you on track.

Hopefully, you can see the power of knowing your desires and then setting goals that align with them. As you achieve your quarterly goals, it can become somewhat addictive as you begin to see progress toward something deeply important to you. Once you start hitting your quarterly goals, you'll also begin to accomplish your annual goals. From there, you may find yourself resetting your goals, making them bigger and more meaningful (yet still achievable) as your confidence in reaching them grows.

Summary

To begin setting goals that align with your lifetime desires, start by identifying those desires and then work backward, creating goals that progressively move you toward them. Break these down into actionable steps by setting three-year, one-year, and quarterly goals. Ensure each goal is Specific, Measurable, Attainable, Relevant, and Timely (SMART). As you achieve your quarterly goals, adjust and refine them as needed to stay on track, building momentum as you move closer to your ultimate vision.

Pro Tip: It's okay for Goals to slide. Sometimes life happens. Sometimes you underestimate how long it takes to complete a goal. No big deal. Keep the goal for the next period and continue to make progress.

To develop your Manifesto #5, visit the how-to section in the book and online at www.madetomatter.coach/manifesto.

– Public Service Announcement –

Growing up, we watched TV over the air, using an antenna. Occasionally, the station would interrupt a show with a Public Service Announcement (PSA), stating, "We interrupt the regularly scheduled program with the following Public Service Announcement." They would then update us on some important news or event—sometimes it was about pending inclement weather, other times, a newsworthy event like the Space Shuttle or Reagan's attempted assassination. It was a signal that it was time to pay attention.

This is this book's PSA, something I want you to know RIGHT NOW:

> Hopefully, the idea of Living a Life That Matters has you excited about the prospect of living your purpose, integrating your passions, using your strengths, setting clear goals, landing your dream job, etc., etc. That is exciting, and you should be excited!
>
> However, the idea of doing all this self-awareness and personal work to make that happen can seem daunting. When it does, you might feel trepidation and fear. I want you to know that's normal.
>
> Rome wasn't built in a day. The contents of this book are the culmination of years and years of research, reading, practicing, and doing my own self-awareness work. It doesn't have to take you that long. That's one reason I wrote the book—to save you from doing all that work I've already done! But there is still work to be done.
>
> Start small. Begin with your Purpose Assessment, as that's the lens through which everything else you

define and uncover should be viewed. Then move on to your values, followed by your strengths. Be diligent, stick with it, but don't try to do everything at once. Trust the process and pace yourself.

Stay excited, knowing that some fear may pop up— that is totally normal (something would be wrong if fear didn't rear its big, nasty head). But commit and see it through. You'll be glad you did!

"And now," as the TV would say: "we return you to your regularly scheduled programming."

Manifesto #6:
Live Your Vision

I will know where I am going and where I want to arrive. I can see that destination clearly in my mind, and I share and invite others to join me.

The classic definition of vision is a desired future state–a destination where you want to arrive on your journey in life. I'm a fan of Andy Stanley's definition of vision in his book, *Visoineering.* Stanley says vision is a "clear mental picture of what could be, fueled by the conviction that it should be."[8]

What is your vision, given that a Life That Matters combines your personal significance, your impact on others, and how your life lived matters to God? What ought it be versus what it is now? What excites you? If you were to dream and develop the exquisite life of which you've always dreamed, what would *that* look like?

For Myself. My vision is that I've truly believed that I am God's masterpiece (Ephesians 2:10), that I've come to understand my calling, and that I've "led a life worthy of my calling, for I have been called by God." (Ephesians 4:1, NLT).

For Others. The vision for my life is that I help 1,000's of people live their purpose. I will encourage them to dig down, take a risk, and put themselves out there. By doing so, they will use their God-given

---

[8] Stanley, A. (1999). *Visioneering: God's Blueprint for Developing and Maintaining Personal Vision.* Multnomah.

talents to produce a better life for themselves, for their loved ones, and those in their life.

For God. And lastly, my vision is that I've lived a life for God, "I have fought the good fight, I have finished the race, I have kept the faith," (2 Timothy 4:6, NLT) and I hear God say, "Well done, my good and faithful servant." (Matthew 25:23a, NLT)

Now, bring it all together. What is a clear, concise vision for my life?

> "I've honored God with how I lived in faith, by living my life to the fullest, and helping thousands of people live their lives to the fullest."

> Let's get it down even simpler:

> "I challenged myself and others to live a life of purpose, in faith, and to the fullest."

At the end of my life, whenever that is, I would hope I would have people stand up to say how Adam Landrum helped them live a Life That Matters. Adam challenged them to step out in faith, to trust the gifts God has given them, and to live life to the fullest.

Even in death, that would be a great day!

Notice how I've written my vision as if it has already happened. This approach is similar to how professional athletes visualize their success. They imagine hitting that ace in tennis, knocking the ball next to the pin in golf, or swishing the game-winning three-pointer in basketball. In the same way, you need to visualize your vision as if it has already come to pass, believing without a doubt that it will happen. When you can do this, having a vision in front of you becomes incredibly powerful. You will start to attract opportunities—some might even say you'll manifest them. In my experience, when you have a clear vision, you subconsciously begin to orient your life towards it. You become aware of what you're striving to achieve, and as a result, you start noticing the things that are important to you. I suspect that these opportunities were always there, but without a vision, you just couldn't see them. Now you can.

Getting your vision set clear as a bell in your mind's eye, will make a huge difference in your life. In fact, I'm willing to bet, it could be one of the biggest contributing factors to living a Life That Matters.

Summary

Now that you've started thinking about your vision, it's time to take action. The next step is to clarify your vision by completing the Future Self Exercise that is available on the website. This exercise will help you solidify a clear, concise vision for your life—a vision that will guide your decisions and actions moving forward.

To get started, visit the website and complete the Future Self Exercise. This will help you begin visualizing your life as if your vision has already been realized, setting you on the path to truly living a Life That Matters.

###

To develop your Manifesto #6, visit the how-to section in the book and online at www.madetomatter.coach/manifesto.

Manifesto #7:
Live Your Current Mission

I will always be on a mission, accomplishing the next milestone in life on my way to realize my vision.

The word "mission" has been heavily misused. Many corporations claim their mission, but what they're often referring to is their purpose (why they exist). Sometimes, mission is even mistaken for vision (where we want to end up, a desired future state).

However, mission is neither of these things. Instead, mission bridges the gap between purpose and vision. A mission is the current strategy or assignment you undertake to move closer to your vision.

Webster defines "mission" as "an important assignment carried out for X." To cement this definition for us, let's think of it in terms of war. Imagine a war, where the ultimate vision is an independent country where people are free. This war comprises many battles, the missions that must be won to win the war.

Consider a particular battle: capturing a specific beachfront. This mission has been meticulously planned for months, requiring significant resources and training. It's not just an isolated task; it's a critical mission with a specific objective to help win the war. Success in this mission is imperative for advancing towards the vision of freedom.

Similarly, your mission is your current, significant assignment, carried out to advance you toward your vision. Ideally, your mission aligns with a three-year goal, though it may be as short-term as a one-year plan. Like the military mission above, your current mission should be substantial—it should stretch you.

Assume you're 40 years old. Think of your vision as the war and your age as the timeline for your battles. If your mission averages 1-3 years, you might have 10-15 missions left to accomplish in your life. This realization is sobering, and that's the point. We need to wake up and get serious about living a Life That Matters! Don't you want to fill the chapters of your life with missions that truly matter?

It's crucial to distinguish between your purpose, mission, and vision. Your purpose—freedom, in our analogy—is constant; it's what you want to see in the world. Your mission, however, changes frequently due to life circumstances and events, and your vision is the ultimate end goal you're striving toward.

Returning to the war analogy, the vision is freedom, the overarching reason for fighting. The war is won through multiple missions, each contributing to the vision. Imagine if a General mistook capturing the beachfront mission for the vision of winning the war. If they succeeded in their mission, the General might prematurely believe they'd won the entire war! But no, the mission was crucial for the war, yet many more missions still need to be executed to achieve victory. Confusing your mission with your vision can be catastrophic to living a Life That Matters.

It's essential to know what your current mission is. Without it, what's guiding your decisions and actions? Your mission is key to living a proactive life, serving as your north star for where to invest your time, money, and energy over the next 1-3 years.

###

If I want to help 1,000's of people courageously live their purpose, then what would my current mission be?

In order to determine that, I have to take stock with where I am and where I need to be. At this time (this is based on a true story, but I'll take some liberties here) this is where I am:

- I'm the CEO of a purpose-driven company that indirectly aligns to my purpose (we help Universities attract more of the right students)
- I'm challenging my teammates at work to own their Super-Genius and to live proactively
- I'm a certified executive coach
- I know my Super-Genius is to challenge people, see into their souls, and ask them questions that give them incredible insights. I love to take people on adventures, challenge them for self-discovery, with the intent to own their purpose (I do this organically, meaning, when I go on trips with people they get challenged)
- I'm married, and have 4 teenagers which means I have precious years left with them and they are also becoming more independent.

My purpose is to challenge people to courageously live their purpose. And my vision is to live by faith, to live and help others live a full, purposeful life.

What should my mission be? Up to this point, I've lived my purpose, almost, indirectly. I want to live my purpose more directly, pointing my life more squarely at my vision.

Therefore, **my current mission is to align my vocation with my purpose and my vision.** I believe that will take me 1-3 years to orient my vocation along those lines.

I will create a strategy to do that. The objectives of that strategy will most likely make it to my 1 and 3 year plan goals.

That's an highlevel overview of how you develop your mission.

Summary

We will look at the components of creating a mission in the How-to section of the book and online.

For now, the main thing I want to get across is the distinction between purpose, mission, and vision. The mission is the exciting how-to that bridges the gap between the two. A mission, like goals, should have a definitive objective. You know when it's accomplished and when the mission is complete, guess what? It's time to set a new mission.

Can you have multiple missions? You could, but I wouldn't recommend it. You'll have many goals in your quarterly, one and three year plans that may not be part of your mission. Your mission keeps you focused on the most important aspect of creating a Life That Matters. Have a mission with a clear objective. Stay on mission. Accomplish your mission. Then rinse and repeat!

To develop your Manifesto #7, visit the how-to section in the book and online at www.madetomatter.coach/manifesto.

Manifesto #8:
Live Using Your
Super-Genius

I will use my Super-Genius as much as possible to maximize my impact for myself and others.

GENIUS

"What's the one thing you are best at?" he asked.

Little did I know, I'd soon find myself in a fetal position for the next two weeks. It was something I'd never considered before, and once I did, it made my brain hurt all over again, like when I was six years old trying to figure out how the universe started. What was I best at? Is there just one thing? If so, shouldn't I already know it? And what if I'm actually not good at the very thing I'm supposed to be best at? I wrestled with these questions—not just over the next two weeks, but for the next two *decades*.

It doesn't have to be that hard. You do have a Super-Genius, and you will find it if you follow the exercises I prescribe for you in the How-to section on the website.

In my experience, "What are you best at?" is one of the most wicked questions out there. I've asked CEOs, university presidents, interview candidates, and coaching clients, and I've watched every one of them squirm. I imagine there's a battle in their minds, something like, "I should know this... but just one thing?... *precious*..." (think Gollum from *Lord of the Rings*).

And now I ask you: What is the one thing you're best at?

Great work has been done around this idea of genius by the Conscious Leadership Group, based out of Chicago. They call it the Zone of Genius. Dan Sullivan, of Toronto-based Strategic Coach®, calls it the Unique Ability®. The concepts are the same. The idea is this: Each of us is gifted in some way that makes us unique. We have talents or abilities to do something better than almost everyone else, and it's relatively effortless for us. In fact, your Super-Genius is so effortless, you don't think it's a big deal. People have probably remarked on how good you are at something, and you've shrugged it off with a dismissive comment like, "Oh, it's nothing."

Except that it is something. It's your Super-Genius.

When you operate in your Super-Genius, you're often in flow. You spend less energy to get things done. Your talent comes naturally to you, and flow is synonymous with being in the zone. You can accomplish tasks at an extremely high level, practically subconsciously.

But as Dr. Seuss says, "Except that you won't because sometimes you don't." There are many reasons that keep us from living in our Super-Genius, and before I list them, I'll give you the number one reason: You. Without a doubt, you are the main reason you don't live in your Super-Genius. And it's because you're scared to.

Imagine telling the world that your Super-Genius is Ice Sculpting (and it truly is), and that you're going to be a world-famous ice sculptor, traveling the lands, practicing your craft. You might think, sure, if I were really a great ice sculptor, that's what I'd do. But it doesn't work that way, right? You'd have to put yourself out there and determine if you can make a living. Hang a shingle as an ice sculptor. Identify as a sculptor. Set up a freezing cold shed to practice and perfect your craft. Learn everything about the industry, be passionate about it, and truly orient your life around it.

It would be cruel to have a Super-Genius but no interest or passion in it. I suspect that could happen, but it's unlikely. When you're good at something, it feels so good to do it that everything in your life tends to gravitate toward it. On the flip side, just because you're great at something doesn't mean it's not still scary to put yourself out there. All too often, the safe path robs us of using our Super-Genius. Hence the famous poem "The Road Not Taken" by Mr. Frost. Every once in a while, take the one less traveled!

Another factor that keeps us from owning our Super-Genius is a sense of responsibility—to keep it up, to not lose it. It's like Superman and Spider-Man, who at some point buckle under the responsibility of having to use their superpowers. It seems most people feel it's easier not to know or use their superpowers; less will be expected of them. As Calvin from Calvin and Hobbes eloquently said to Susie, "I find my life is a lot easier the lower I keep everyone's expectations."

Why don't leaders such as university presidents, CEOs, or those I interview or coach know their Super-Genius? Because they don't want the responsibility of having to live it out. So instead of standing in their Super-Genius, they settle for a step down: in their Excellence. And while that's not a bad place to be, it's not their Super-Genius. It's like getting second place, which is also known as "first loser." Or like winning the silver medal instead of the gold. Second fiddle. Runner-up. In horse racing, not win, but place—second place. You get the picture. We try to be nice about getting second, but we all want to win. Living in your Super-Genius is winning. Living in anything else is, well: second place, runner-up, nice try—aka losing.

Many of us operate in our Excellence. We're pretty good at these things—better than most, actually. We do a good job. It's of some interest to us. We're not in flow, but we can do these activities with minimal effort. However, unlike your Super-Genius, it does take some effort!

It gets worse, unfortunately. We also operate at some level of competence or incompetence. At competence, sure, we can do it, but it's not going to be great (that would be yardwork for me). As for incompetence, we're not good at it. We're actually bad at it, and we shouldn't be doing it at all. My zone of incompetence would be fixing appliances—washing machines, dryers, refrigerators, etc. Do not give Adam a set of tools and tell him to fix anything. It will end up worse than he found it! My wife has officially banned me from even thinking about repairing an appliance.

The reality is that sometimes we have to do competent or even incompetent tasks. I have four children, and consoling a baby was neither my Super-Genius nor at my Excellence level. My wife, on the other hand, was quite good at it. But there were times and nights when I was the one doing the consoling. So be it—I did the best I could within my level of competence (sorry, kids).

So what do we do if we find that we're not operating at our level of Super-Genius?

Moving up the staircase is what we do. When you shift most of your activities and efforts toward your Super-Genius, you start providing more value, gain more energy, and become a better teammate, partner, friend, etc. You're doing what you were made to do, and that makes you more fulfilled—a Life That Matters.

Summary

Knowing and living your Super-Genius is key to living a Life That Matters because it lets you do what you're naturally great at. When you operate in your Super-Genius, you're in flow, feeling energized, and making a bigger impact. Instead of settling for just being good at something, you push yourself to excel, which leads to a more meaningful and fulfilling life.

In the How-to section of the book and website, you'll find an exercise designed to help you identify your strengths and rank them as your Super-Genius. This process will guide you in aligning your activities and efforts with your unique talents, allowing you to provide more value, gain more energy, and ultimately contributing to live a Life That Matters.

###

To develop your Manifesto #8, visit the how-to section in the book and online at www.madetomatter.coach/manifesto.

Manifesto #9: Live with a Vocational Alignment

I will have an occupation that allows me to use my Super-Genius and is aligned with the other components of my Life That Matters Manifesto.

You've most likely heard the cliché: "If you love what you do, you'll never work another day in your life."

Yet so few of us realize this principle, as Gallup reports that 68% of Americans are not engaged at work[9]. This is a sad statistic, especially since we spend more than half of our waking hours at work rather than at home. Imagine how much more meaningful life would be if you loved your work. So, why don't those 100 million+ disengaged people go find a job they would love?

One's vocation should be a major building block in creating a Life That Matters, but many people are searching for a dream job before understanding their purpose, vision, and mission. They're getting the cart before the horse. Sure, the grass may seem greener on the other side, but it often isn't—especially if you haven't done the work of establishing your foundation of a Life That Matters.

Knowing your purpose and values should guide the type of employer you work for. Knowing your vision and current mission will likely

---

[9] Harter, J. (2023, January 25). U.S. Employee Engagement Needs a Rebound in 2023. Gallup. https://www.gallup.com/workplace/468233/employee-engagement-needs-rebound-2023.aspx

inform the kind of role you take on. For instance, if you're the primary caregiver of four small children at home, taking a job that requires you to be on the road 80% of the time probably isn't a great idea. A properly aligned vocation is key to living a Life That Matters, but the foundation must be laid first, or the dream job will remain just that—a dream.

Similar to The Life That Matters hierarchy, there's a hierarchy to a vocation that matters (which could be a book within itself). Here are the four levels, based on the Life That Matters Hierarchy:

1. **Believe in your Job.** Your job and the organization you work for aligns with your personal values.
2. **Love your job.** Passions align with the job.
3. **Live in the Zone.** Your Super-Genius is the primary skills/talents you use for your job.
4. **A Higher Job.** Your job allows you to be aligned with your purpose, a cause you have adopted, or your higher calling.

To make your job matter so your life matters more, first, work for a company you respect and values what you value. For instance, if you don't value consumer debt, then working for a credit card company or a payday loan company probably wouldn't be a good fit. There's nothing inherently wrong with those companies, but if they don't align with your values, it makes sense to look for work elsewhere. Don't work for a company that doesn't align with your values. But take it one step further—do work for a company that does align with your values!

Like the Life That Matters Hierarchy, you don't necessarily have to follow these steps in order. However, to gain more fulfillment in life, your work should be something you love. At the very least, have a job or career that you're passionate about.

Next, do something where you can use your gifts and flex your Super-Genius. This will make your career much more enjoyable and impactful. You'll be a star player on the team, elevating everyone else's performance. Plus, you'll make a bigger contribution to your company, and when you're more valuable to your company, you're typically rewarded for that value.

Think about it. Do you work for an organization that you respect and feel aligned with its values? (Now, if you haven't defined your own values, be careful how you judge here!) Are you in a role where you love what you do—experiencing passion and fulfillment—and are using your Super-Genius gifts? If not, do you believe that opportunity is out there? And if so, wouldn't you do whatever it takes to get that type of job?

Let's take it a step further because we're after all interested in living a Life That Matters. What if you could get a bit greedier (as if this job isn't already awesome)? What if your job aligned with your purpose? And even more, aligned with your vision?

Oh, come on, Adam, now you're getting ridiculous! Am I? Okay, I'd be happy if you at least did something you loved. I'd be happy if you did something where you could use your gifts. You'd be in the super-minority that not only chose to find a fulfilling job but actually made it happen.

I'd really be impressed if you went all out and pursued a purpose-driven vocation that aligned with your values, personal purpose, Super-Genius, passions, and vision. Perhaps it even aligned with your cause and/or your higher power's purpose.

It's up to you how much you want to optimize your vocation. Again, you can focus on one level of vocational alignment, and that will make your life matter more. Or you can do all four! Here they are again:

1. **Believe in your Job.** Your job and the organization you work for aligns with your personal values
2. **Love your job.** Several passions align with your job.

3. **Super-Genius Job.** Your Super-Genius is the primary skills/talents you use for your job.

4. **A Higher Job.** Your job allows you to be aligned with your purpose, the cause you have adopted, and/or your higher calling.

If you feel that all four are unrealistic, then you're right. Don't try it. Don't go for it. Leave that for the dreamers. But if there's even a sliver of doubt—if you think that dream job or career might be out there, and the risk to find it and do it might be worth it—let me leave you with some sobering feedback from author Adam Grant:

> *"If you're considering a career change but worried about taking a step backward, remember this: It's better to lose the past 2 years of progress than to waste the next 20."*

Summary

We've talked about how aligning your job with your values, passions, Super-Genius, and vision can make your life more meaningful. It's not easy, but if you believe your dream job is out there, it's worth chasing.

###

To develop your Manifesto #9, visit the how-to section in the book and online at www.madetomatter.coach/manifesto.

Manifesto #10:
Serving a Cause

I will serve something larger than me, choosing to serve a cause or movement that I am passionate about.

A cause is a movement that, because of deep conviction, you're prepared to defend or advocate for.

A cause gives a person tremendous energy. When you believe in something so strongly that you're willing to sacrifice your time, money, and talents to serve and progress the movement, that's powerful—and that's living a Life That Matters.

There are countless causes out there. Some already exist; others need to be created. Maybe living a Life That Matters means you're going to start a cause that the world is asking for?

While there are many causes I don't personally align with, I respect those who are so passionate about their cause that they're willing to live—or even lose—their lives for it. There are opposing causes, and that's okay. Many causes oppose each other, as they should, given our differing beliefs. One person might be for women's rights, while another is for babies' rights. There are those against guns and those for guns. Many people are passionate about their political parties, with great people on both sides of the aisle.

It's not the specific cause that matters most, but the fact that you have one. Your job, if you choose to accept it, is to pick the one you want your life to support.

Let me take a quick timeout here. Believing in a cause and actually being part of a cause are two different things. Social media has amplified many opinions with little action. I'm glad you're passionate about something and have a strong opinion, but unless you're actively participating in the cause, you're not contributing to a Life That Matters. You're just screaming. And it's annoying. So, please stop it.

If you believe strongly in "your" cause, then I expect you to give financially (in a way that stings), dedicate copious amounts of your time, and roll up your sleeves to get dirty.

Those who truly believe in something walk the talk and put their money where their mouth is. When you live for a cause, you make your life matter.

Summary

Having a cause gives you the energy and purpose to live a Life That Matters. It's not just about believing in something—it's about rolling up your sleeves and getting involved. If you're passionate about a cause but haven't jumped in yet, make it a goal to volunteer this quarter. If you don't have a cause, set a goal to find one by the end of the year that aligns with your values and desires.

###

To develop your Manifesto #10, visit the how-to section in the book and online at www.madetomatter.coach/manifesto.

Manifesto #11:
Live for a Higher Calling

I will seek out my higher calling and orient my life to that calling to accomplish the God-given mission I am given.

Alright, let's talk about your higher calling. Now, this isn't a required component for living a Life That Matters, but here's something I've noticed: the people I know who are truly living a Life That Matters all have one thing in common. They're living their lives for a higher power—they believe in a creator, something much bigger than themselves. These people have aligned their lives so closely with this higher power that they would call it a calling—a higher calling.

Plain and simple, a person with a higher calling is someone on a mission for God.

When we think of people who are really living a Life That Matters, we often picture missionary types, right? People who have oriented their lives around something deeply profound, at least to them. They feel like they're serving someone else, serving this higher power for a purpose. Because of that, they're willing to make great sacrifices in their lives to serve that higher power and answer their higher calling.

However, like in my story earlier in the book, I realized I didn't need to be a "missionary" or be in the mission field to live my higher calling. I know many businesspeople who feel their higher calling is to tell other businesspeople about God. And for those who are interested, they're willing to mentor them. Business people also play the role of financing the priests of their higher calling.

A higher calling doesn't mean you're moving to Africa and taking a vow of poverty for the rest of your life. It means you believe in a higher power and are either taking on another mission (from God) or replacing your personal mission with His. The most aligned Life That Matters would have a purpose, vision, mission, and vocation all directed toward God. As a wise man recently put it to me, "I live my life *ruthlessly* for God."

HIGHER CALLING

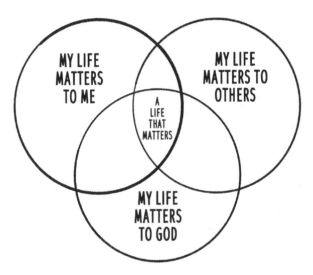

So how do you know what your higher calling is if you don't know a higher power? And if you want a higher calling, how do you get one?

A Higher Power

To believe in a higher power, you have to choose to have faith in that power. A higher calling will require faith at some level, period. Faith is simply "believing in the unseen." Ultimately, you have to believe in the concept of faith itself. And believing in faith means you have to jump—the bridge won't magically come together. The chasm won't close just so you can waltz across. You have to let go, trust, and believe that the Higher Power is who and what He says He is, and believe that unconditionally.

If you were raised in the church and deep down you know that the Judeo-Christian faith is the way—you believe in the Trinity, the doctrine of sin, grace, and redemption, but maybe you've just been too stubborn to believe—then I encourage you to just believe. Just do it. You won't have all the answers, and you never will. That's the point. That's faith. A quote I saw on a coffee cup sums it up nicely: "God is under NO obligation to make sense to you."

Candidly, I can't speak to other religions. But just as a Christian may have been raised in a Christian home, you may have been raised in a Hindu household or by Buddhist parents. Or maybe you've flirted with believing in an omnipotent "Universe." Personally, I believe in one God, a creator, who sent His son to die a sacrificial death so you could be with God for eternity. But that's just what I believe. What I'm encouraging you to do is fully believe in whatever higher power you believe in. And once you believe, throw your life into that belief. If it really is a Higher Power, then don't you think that power is worth living for?

A Higher Calling

Once you believe in a higher power, I simply believe your God will give you a mission. In the Judeo-Christian faith, Jesus reiterated commands like the Great Commandment and the Golden Rule. These are principles to follow, and they could form a significant part of your higher calling. Loving God with all your heart, mind, soul, and strength is a pretty stout calling. And He adds more through the Golden Rule: Love your neighbor as yourself. What a standard! We love ourselves quite a bit, don't we? In His last days, Jesus gave His disciples a mission: Go to the corners of the earth and make disciples of all nations.

If you're a Christian, it's hard to think you don't have that calling by default. The question is, will God get more specific? Will He say go to Africa, or disciple businesspeople, or work for that church, or support an orphanage, or foster children? I don't know, but if you believe in a higher power, you should be looking for your higher calling. "I beg you to lead a life worthy of your calling, for you have been called by God." —Ephesians 4:1.

How Do You Get Your Calling?

From a Christian standpoint, you can get a calling in several ways. You might "hear" directly from God (it's usually not audible, but through prayer), be spoken to through reading scripture, have a sense of direction from the Holy Spirit, or receive confirmation from other people. God can work in many mysterious ways, but those are the most common.

Now listen, I understand this may sound ridiculous. I get it. But remember, believing in a higher power takes faith, even when it doesn't make sense.

I currently don't have a missional higher calling, but I do believe God told me to move to Greenville, SC. At the time, we were living in a suburb of Atlanta, and I heard Him say, "Go to Greenville." So my wife, two toddlers, a newborn, and I relocated to the area. Concerned about whether my young agency would thrive, we bought a more affordable house in a small town outside the city. After a couple of years, I grew discontent with the neighborhood and the long commute I'd given myself. One morning, during that commute, as I crested a hill with a beautiful view of the mountains, God clearly said to me, "I said GREENVILLE."

Even though we couldn't afford a house downtown, I moved forward in faith. We got our house ready to sell, searched for a new one in the city, and God provided the perfect place that was close to downtown. We listed our current home, bought the new one, and promptly moved in.

I don't know the specifics of why God wants me in Greenville, but I'm here. Sometimes you don't have a clear understanding or picture of what He's up to. That's called faith. In the meantime, while I'm where He told me to be, I have the Great Commandment (love your God), the Golden Rule (love your neighbor), and the Great Commission (make disciples) to guide me and keep me on track with my Higher Power.

Summary

I've talked about how faith and listening to a higher power can guide you to where you're meant to be, even when it doesn't make sense, requiring faith. If you're trying to find your higher calling or want to align your life more with your faith, head over to the How-to section on the website. You'll find exercises and guidance to help you discover and pursue your own higher calling.

###

To develop your Manifesto #11, visit the how-to section in the book and online at www.madetomatter.coach/manifesto.

The Life That Matters Workbook

This workbook will help you implement what you have learned in *The Life That Matters Manifesto*. We've talked quite a bit about theory and concepts. Now it's time to put it to practice. Roll up your sleeves. It's time to go to work and start peeling back the onion to discover what your Life that Matters will look like!

You'll have opportunities to use some tools, put the concepts to work, take some assessments and document the ingredients of your life to begin shaping that delicious dish we call a Life that Matters!

NOW, MAKE YOUR LIFE MATTER, MORE

Manifesto #1: Purpose How-To

Concept Review

Your purpose is why you exist. You are uniquely made, and the sum of your parts makes you a fabulous, one-of-a-kind human being. You're on this earth for a reason, with a purpose that's meant to be fulfilled.

I hope that doesn't scare you, but as the saying goes, "You are fearfully and wonderfully made."

I believe your purpose was in you before you were born. It's been shaped and refined by your personality, circumstances, Super-Genius, and more. All these elements work together to help define your purpose.

You've probably been living out your purpose since you were very young. But for some of us, we've been told to stop living our purpose—maybe because we were too overbearing with it, or because we didn't fit in, so the group pulled us back down. Sometimes, our purpose gets sidetracked by others, like well-meaning parents with different aspirations for their children.

The main reason we don't live our purpose is because of ourselves. We're scared to live it out. Like we discussed in the Super-Genius chapter: What if I fail? What if living my purpose means I have to become a missionary? What if I can't make enough money doing it? There are countless reasons to hesitate, but let's put those aside for now. Let's uncover your purpose, and then you can decide how you want to respond to those questions and what you want to do with it.

Purposeful Passion

Step 1. Purpose Questions. Please answer the following questions with no or little thought. Shoot from the hip, answer them from your gut. Go with whatever comes to mind.

1. What did you most enjoy doing as a kid more than anything else?
2. What brings tears to your eyes that normally don't make others cry?
3. What topic or subject makes you pound the table with your fists, gets you so fired up, you practically have a visceral response to the topic?
4. What gives you goosebumps?
5. When's a time you've been in the zone or in flow and what were you doing?
6. What's something you got in trouble for as a kid, though it's what naturally flowed from you?
7. If people who knew you well were to describe your essence, what would they say that is?
8. If your best friend had to say what your purpose is, what would he or she say?

As an example, here's Mark's exercise. It took him about 90 seconds to record his top of "gut" responses:

1. What did you most enjoy doing as a kid more than anything else?
   Leading things competitively. I loved to win, and turned everything into a competition. And I also just assumed I was the leader and so I led.

2. What brings tears to your eyes that normally don't make others cry?
Life change. When people get baptized at church, my eyes well up. I can't help it or stop it.

3. What topic or subject makes you pound the table with your fists, gets you so fired up, you practically have a visceral response to the topic?
When the innocent and defenseless get taken advantage of. Orphans, sex-trafficking.

4. What gives you goosebumps?
People who help people elevate by depending on God. The biography of William Booth, the founder of the Salvation Army. His faith and dependence on God is legendary and the number of people he's impacted is countless.

5. When's a time you've been in the zone or in flow?
Sports many times. But now, teaching. When I'm teaching people who are hungry and want to succeed, I could teach forever.

6. What's something you got in trouble for as a kid, though it's what naturally flowed from you?
A kid at school was getting bullied. Without thinking twice, I walked him home to make sure the bully didn't follow. His house was in the opposite direction of mine, and I ended up getting home about 90 minutes later than I should have. My mom was fit to be tied—so upset that even when I explained why I was late, it didn't calm her down. I felt she was wrong and I was right. The unintended lesson I learned was that I was going to double down on doing the right thing, even if it meant breaking the rules. I'd do it again, of course, but I've always been disappointed that my parents didn't see what I did for that kid as "good." I understood

why my mom was upset, but I thought she should have seen the bigger picture.

7. If people who knew you well were to describe your essence, what would they say that is?
   They would say I care about people, I want to see people succeed—including my wife and kids of course, and that I'm sold out for God.

8. If your best friend had to say what your purpose is, what would they say?
   He would say, Mark exists to make people better.

Step 2. Take the Purpose Essence Assessment.

www.madetomatter.coach/manifesto

Record the results here: _____

Respond:

How do you feel your Purpose Essence is true about you?

Step 3. Take the Enneagram Assessment (Free)

The Enneagram is one of the most introspective and revealing personality assessments I've taken. We use it in Conscious Leadership at my company, and it's gaining popularity worldwide. While rooted in ancient traditions, the Enneagram was modernized by Oscar Ichazo[10] in the 1960's.

My interpretation of the Enneagram is that our personalities are driven by unconscious fears and desires that shape our beliefs, feelings, and actions. If we're unaware of these fears and desires, our personalities can become unhealthy. But if we're conscious of them, we can tap into our strengths and develop a very healthy personality.

For instance, I am an Enneagram 8, also known as the Challenger. My main fear is being taken advantage of or harmed. My primary desire is a lust—not necessarily sexual, but a lust for deep intensity with people and life in general.

When I'm unhealthy, I walk around in my armor, always keeping an eye on the horizon. I'll smite anything that poses a threat, whether perceived or real. It's an exhausting way to live and quite unhealthy. I'm making no political statement here, but in my opinion, Donald Trump is an example of a very unhealthy Enneagram 8.

When healthy, an Eight integrates into the Enneagram 2 (The Helper) and becomes a tremendous lover, protector, and friend. He realizes the world is not out to get him, allowing him to let his guard down and use his immense core of power and strength to love others. Presumed healthy 8s include Franklin D. Roosevelt and Winston Churchill[11].

---

[10] https://www.integrative9.com/enneagram/history/
[11] http://www.refreshleadership.com/index.php/2020/05/leading-numbers-enneagram-leader-type-8-challenger/

That's merely just a sample and the tip of the iceberg. I'll warn you, it's a rabbit hole, but worth the trip. Here's the free assessment I'd encourage you to take: https://www.eclecticenergies.com/enneagram/dotest

Your Enneagram Type: _____

When you are at your healthiest, what does your type typically do (copy from the assessment results)?

How much do you agree with this and or how does that apply to you?

Step 4. Record Your Purpose Statement.

Using your intuition, your answers from the purpose questions, the purpose assessment, and insights from the Enneagram, record the *essence* of your purpose below (don't worry about getting your purpose statement perfect. Getting to the essence is the objective).

My purpose, the reason I exist is to:

Example, Mark:

Purpose Assessment: Helping Heart

Enneagram: 3 with a 2 wing. (Achiever/Helper, called the "The Charmer")

They inspire others to keep moving, keep trying, keep doing things. They make others believe that success is possible and that they, too, can have it all.

Purpose: To help people who want to be better.

Recap

Again, don't overthink it. Trust your gut based on the answers you provided above. Don't get caught up in wordsmithing your purpose statement—focus on understanding the essence. On the one-page Life That Matters worksheet we provide online, you'll write down your purpose-essence and review it frequently to remind yourself why you're here and what you're here to do. Over time, you can refine it, find the right words, make it more concise, and so on. But for now, just bask in the essence of your purpose. Well done!

For these tools and additional resources to develop Manifesto #1, visit www.madetomatter.coach/manifesto.

Manifesto #2: Values - How To

Concept Review

Values are what you truly prioritize. Often called Core Values, they're the top 3-7 principles that guide your decisions and choices, subtly (or not so subtly) directing your life. Remember, there's a difference between what we say we value and what we actually value. A great way to determine your real values is to audit where you spend your time, money, and energy.

So What do you value?

The most effective way I've helped people uncover their values is by having them brainstorm a list of things they value. And remember the #1 rule of brainstorming: No judgment. Just let your thoughts flow freely—everything from 'Honesty' to 'my iPhone' is fair game. Once you've got your list, go through it and group similar values together. The goal is to narrow it down to 3-7 core values. Also, consider where you spend your time and money—these are often, for better or worse, great indicators of what you truly value.

1. Where do I spend the most time outside of work and sleep?

   ----

2. What do I spend the most money on outside of rent/mortgage?

   ----

3. Where do I serve and give of my efforts?

Don't be discouraged if you don't have great answers right now—that's okay. Instead, consider what you wish you could answer as true. Why? Because this will provide you with another piece of the puzzle in discovering what truly matters to you!

A Special Note: Values that Don't "Count"

There are types of values that I encourage you not to "count" or consider:

Table stake Values - Values like honesty, integrity, and character are important, but don't you expect everyone in your life to embody these qualities? If they don't, they're simply not the kind of people you want to associate with, right? I have a saying: if someone has to tell you they're honest—watch out. Rule out these baseline values. They're implied and don't need to be stated.

Aspirational Values - These values are aspirational in nature, much like the woman I described in Manifesto #2. She was drawn to the idea of being purpose-driven or serving others, but her actions didn't reflect these values in her life. We don't want to create a list of values we hope to aspire to; instead, we're creating a list of values that we actually live by.

Values Exercise

Below is a list of values you may want to consider using for your values brainstorm. We'll use this list for Mark's examples below.

Values (adapted from jamesclear.com)

Authenticity	Happiness	Pleasure
Adventure	Impact	Poise
Autonomy	Influence	Popularity
Balance	Inner Harmony	Recognition
Compassion	Justice	Religion
Community	Kindness	Reputation
Creativity	Knowledge	Respect
Curiosity	Leadership	Responsibility
Determination	Learning	Security
Fairness	Love	Self-Respect
Faith	Loyalty	Service
Fame	Meaningful Work	Spirituality
Friendships	Openness	Stability
Fun	Optimism	Success
Growth	Peace	Status
		Trustworthiness
		Wealth
		Wisdom

Step 1. Brainstorm Your Values. Create a list of all of the things you value. Feel free to add examples from the list above.

Mark's Example Values:

Authenticity	**Happiness**	~~Pleasure~~
Adventure	**Impact**	~~Poise~~
Autonomy	**Influence**	~~Popularity~~
Balance	**Inner Harmony**	~~Recognition~~
~~Compassion~~	**Justice**	~~Religion~~
~~Community~~	~~Kindness~~	~~Reputation~~
~~Creativity~~	~~Knowledge~~	**Respect**
Curiosity	**Leadership**	**Responsibility**
Determination	**Learning**	~~Security~~
~~Fairness~~	**Love**	~~Self-Respect~~
Faith	~~Loyalty~~	~~Service~~
~~Fame~~	**Meaningful Work**	**Spirituality**
Friendships	**Openness**	~~Stability~~
Fun	**Optimism**	**Success**
Growth	~~Peace~~	~~Status~~
		Trustworthiness
		~~Wealth~~
		Wisdom

Round 2: Grouping. From your list of values, group those that are similar. Mark grouped his values as follows:

Authenticity	Curiosity	Respect
Openness	Learning	Trustworthiness
Love	Growth	Responsibility
Family	Wisdom	
Friendships		
	Spirituality	
Adventure	Faith	~~Justice~~[7]
Fun	Happiness	
	Inner Harmony	
Leadership	Balance	
Autonomy		
Determination	Meaningful Work	
	Impact	
	Influence	
	Success	

---

[12] This gave Mark 7 groups. He could go with that, but he wonders if he could simplify more. Also, he noticed "Justice" was hanging out there by itself, so he determined it just wasn't a core value and he eliminated it.

Step 3: Title Your Groups. Give your groups a title name. Select one of the values in the group that represents the group the best, and come up with a meaningful title for the group. See Mark's example below.

Authentic Relationships	**Curious Learner**	**Make a Difference**
Openness	Learning	Meaningful Work
Love	Growth	Impact
Family	Wisdom	Influence
Friendships	Adventure	Success
	Fun	
		Radically
Lead to Potential	**Believe**	**Responsible**
Autonomy	Faith Spirituality	Respect
Determination	Happiness	Trustworthiness
	Inner Harmony	
	Balance	

Note: Mark still has six value groups. But note that now they are grouped, he named them in a way that are meaningful and memorable and represent the core values in each group.

Step 4: Create Your Values Narrative. Write a short description of what that value means to you, so that it's consistent with the original values that comprised the group.

Values	Value Narrative
Authentic Relationships	I have meaningful relationships with friends and family, where I am myself and I love others for being who they are.
Lead to Potential	I have a created a life that gives me the flexibility to lead a life striving toward my potential and I encourage and lead others who are open to living their potential
Curious Learner and Teacher	I am a continual learner, deepening my knowledge of subjects I know, learning new subjects, sharing what I learn through teaching, trying new experiences, and love enjoying an adventure with loved ones and looking forward to the next!
Believe	I believe there is no impossible, there are 1,000 ways to get something done, and that God is in control of the world and my life, period.
Make a Difference	I do things with a purpose, to make a difference, or I don't spend time and energy doing it.
Radically Responsible	You can count on me to do what I said I will do. I am completely trustworthy and dependable.

Note: Mark used all of the remaining values as grouped, and then wrote the following narratives to make his values come to life.

Recap

To uncover your true values, start by brainstorming a list of everything you value—without judgment. Group similar values together and narrow them down to your top 3-7 core values. Remember to focus on values you actively live by, not just those you aspire to. Consider where you spend your time and money, as these are strong indicators of what truly matters to you. This probably seems like a lot when you read it through the steps, but it actually is an exercise that should take you about 60 minutes. Here's a summary of the steps.

Step 1. Brainstorm (10 minutes)

Step 2. Group (10 minutes)

Step 3. Title (these become your top 3-7 values) (10 minutes)

Step 4. Narrative. (15 minutes)

Don't worry if it takes you less or more time—I'm simply providing the time estimates as a guideline. I encourage you to take as much time as you need; just follow through and complete the exercise. I promise, the time and brainpower you invest will be worth it!

###

For these tools and additional resources to develop Manifesto #2, visit www.madetomatter.coach/manifesto.

Manifesto #3: Discovering Your Passions

Concept Review

Living your passions is essential to fueling a Life that Matters. Your passions are the activities you love and that energize you. It's important to identify your passions and, more challenging still, to make sure you're engaging in them regularly.

Know Your Passions

To assist you, I've provided an extensive list of potential passions below. Keep in mind, this list isn't exhaustive—there are undoubtedly passions not included here, like origami, chess, or speed skating, for example.

Step 1. Write a "C" next for the passions that you CURRENTLY love AND do.

Step 2. Write a "P" for the passions that you used to love and do in the PAST.

Step 3. Write an "F" for the passions that you would like to do in the FUTURE.

Health and Wellbeing	Learning and Growing	Work and Service
Healthy eating	Researching	Business and
Walking or hiking	Reading self-help	entrepreneurship
Running	books or taking online	Mentoring
Biking	courses	Leadership
Swimming	Learning new skills	Coaching
Martial Arts	Journalling	Training or teaching
Sports	Gaining Knowledge	Donating
Weights	Gaining Wisdom	Volunteering
Yoga	Personal finance	Worshiping
Meditation		
Massage		
Creative Living	Watching (movies, TV	Love and
Writing	series, documentaries)	Relationships
Speaking	Listening (to music,	Being a Grandparent
Painting, drawing, or	podcasts, audiobooks)	Being a spouse/
crafting	Reviewing	partner
Knitting and	Making and	Being a parent
Crocheting	composing	Being a son/daughter
Designing	Photography	Being a brother/sister
Creating or Editing	Event hosting or	Being a friend
Building or repairing	celebration	Being a relative
Collecting or	Programming	Being a citizen
organizing	Playing or gaming	
Decluttering or	Cooking	
cleaning	Gardening	
Playing an instrument	Animals	
Singing	Nature	
Dancing	Travel	
Acting or	Adventure sports	
entertainment		
Reading fiction		

Step 4. Joy Giving. On a scale of 1 - 10, write next to our passion how much joy/energy doing that passion gave, currently gives, or you think would give you

Step 5. Prioritize your Passions. In the list below, write down the passions by order of joy they give you. Ignore the time/effort column for now.

Step 6. Rank the Effort. On a scale of 1-10, rank how easy/convenient/effortless it is to do that passion (with a 10 being effortless and a 1 expensive/time consuming). For instance, playing a round of golf may be a 5 vs. reading fiction at a 9).

Step 7. Frequency. Indicate the frequency that you feel you could realistically perform that passion. (D)aily, (W)eekly, (M)onthly, (Q)uarterly, (S)emi-Annually, (Y)early, (A)nnually+.

Step 8. Rank your passions by prioritizing your top 10 based on Joy, Effort, and Frequency. Subjectively rank them from 1 to 10 using these three criteria. For example, a passion that brings you 8 Joy, requires only 1 Effort, and can be done daily would rank higher than a passion that gives you 9 Joy but requires 7 Effort and is only done annually. I'd prioritize the easier and more frequent passion higher.

Passion Planning

Rank	Passion	Joy (1-10)	Effort (1-10)	Frequency

Mark's Example:
Note, for formatting purposes, we use bold instead of a circle

Current Passion = C
Past Passion = P
Future Passion = F
Not a Passion = strikethrough

Health and Wellbeing	Learning and Growing	Work and Service
C - Healthy eating	~~Researching~~	**F** - Business and entrepreneurship
C - Walking or hiking	**C** - Reading self-help books or taking online courses	**C** - Mentoring
C - Running	**C** - Learning new skills	**P/F** - Leadership
C - Biking	**C** - Journalling	~~Coaching~~
~~Swimming~~	**C** - Gaining Knowledge	**C** - Training or teaching
~~Martial Arts~~	**C** - Gaining Wisdom	**C** - Donating
C - Sports	~~Personal finance~~	**C** - Volunteering
C - Weights		**C** - Worshiping
~~Yoga~~		
C - Meditation		
~~Massage~~		

Creative Living	Love and Relationships	Not Listed or More Specific
F - Writing	**F** -Being a Grandparent	
F - Speaking		**C** -Golf
~~Painting, drawing, or crafting~~	**C** - Being a spouse/ partner	**C**- Tennis
~~Knitting and Crocheting~~	**C** - Being a parent	**C** -Marriage
~~Designing~~	**C** - Being a son/ daughter	**C** -Physical Therapy
~~Creating or Editing~~		
~~Building or repairing~~	**C** -Being a brother/ sister	
~~Collecting or organizing~~	**C** - Being a friend	
~~Decluttering or cleaning~~	~~Being a relative~~	
~~Playing an instrument~~	~~Being a citizen~~	
~~Singing~~		
~~Dancing~~		
~~Acting or entertainment~~		
C - Reading fiction		
~~Watching (movies, TV series, documentaries)~~		
C- Listening (to music, podcasts, audiobooks)		
~~Making and composing~~		
P - Photography		
C - Event hosting or celebration		

P - Programming **C** - Playing or gaming ~~Cooking~~ ~~Gardening~~ **C** - Animals **C** - Nature **C** -Travel ~~Adventure sports~~		

Passion Planning

Rank	Passion	Joy (1-10)	Effort (1-10)	Frequency
	Healthy Eating	7	5	D
	Hiking	7	5	M
3	Running	9	2	D
	Biking	7	3	M
4	Working Out	9	4	D
9	Golf	9	6	W
	Tennis	8	4	W
2	Teaching	10	5	W
10	Writing	8	5	W
	Speaking	7	6	Q
	Music (Listen)	7	1	W
	Podcast (Listen)	7	1	W
	Read Fiction	7	2	D

8	Read Self Help	8	3	W
1	Marriage	9	3	D
6	Father	8	5	D
	Journalling	7	3	D
7	Mentoring	9	7	M
5	Travel	10	8	S

Interpreting the results:

Mark ranked his passions subjectively, using the inputs of Joy, Effort (time, money, energy), and Frequency to determine each passion's rank. This exercise is about being honest, not politically correct. For instance, Mark ranked "Father" as 6th because, while rewarding, being a father doesn't always provide daily joy and energy. The same could be said for marriage, but for Mark, he and his wife have worked on their marriage to the point where it brings him joy daily. The key is to avoid thinking, "I should value this passion more than another," and ranking it accordingly. Another example is "Healthy Eating." While Mark might feel it should rank higher, it's more of a discipline and lifestyle for him, not necessarily a joy-driven passion, even though he finds some satisfaction in it.

Here are Mark's passions that he's committed to living:

Marriage (D), Teaching (W), Running (D), Working Out(D), Travel(S), Father(D), Mentoring(W), Reading Self Help(W), Golf(W), Writing(W).

And those are just his top 10. He'll also hike once a month, play tennis weekly, read fiction nightly, listen to music, and more. But if he stays disciplined about his passions and lives proactively, his "cup will overflow" with joy and energy, enabling him to effectively impact others.

Recap

Well done, you've identified your passions! Now what? It's time to start living them! Schedule your activities around your passions and commit to them. Use the upcoming goal-setting section to align your goals with your passions.

For these tools and additional resources to develop Manifesto #3, visit www.madetomatter.coach/manifesto.

Manifesto #4 and #5: Desires and Goals

Concept Review - Desires

What do you want for your life? These are your desires. And I used desires vs. goals to delineate the two. As I mentioned in chapter 7, desires are more like ideals that you strive to meet. They are qualitative in nature. A desire may be you want to be a good husband—no—a great husband! That sounds wonderful...and good luck! That's a desire that you may define (what does it mean to be a great father?), will set up goals, and proactively work towards. Being a great husband or wife is something one will never arrive at and will be striving towards one's whole life.

Let's begin articulating our desires. In the table below, circle the things that are important to you. Like the values exercise, group those together as necessary. And then in step 3, prioritize those desires to get to a final recommended list of 3-7. Just a reminder, these are not goals. Goals are something you can reach and check off (i.e. Retire. That is a quantitative goal).

Step 1. Select as many items below that you feel apply to you and feel free to add some of your own as well.

Husband / Wife	Spiritual	Your Own:
Father / Mother	God	
Son / Daughter	Church	
Grandparent		
Friend	Giving	
	Serving / Volunteer	
Financial	Faith	
Physical	Prayer	
Active	Worship	
Healthy		
Professionally	Travel	
Sports	Experiences	
Artistically / Author		
	Cause: _____	
Learn	Mentor	
Wisdom / Knowledge	Coach	

Mark's Example:

Husband / ~~Wife~~	**Spiritual**	Your Own:
Father / ~~Mother~~	**God**	
Son / Daughter	~~Church~~	
Grandparent		
Friend	**Giving**	
	Serving / Volunteer	
Financial	**Faith**	
Physical	~~Prayer~~	
Active	~~Worship~~	
Healthy		
Professionally	Travel	
Sports	Experiences	
Artistically / Author		
	Cause: _____	
Learn	Mentor	
Wisdom / Knowledge	Coach	

Step 2. Group your Desires. Look at the list above? Can you group any same or similar desires (e.g. Mark combined (Physical, Healthy and Active into one desire just called "Healthy." He also combined Financial and Giving into a desire called "Generous")

Group like-desires here:

Mark's Example:

Husband	Giving
	Serving / Volunteer
Father	
	Spiritual
Friend	God
	Faith
Physical	
Active	

Step 3. Prune. If you have more than seven desires, ask yourself if any can be combined or eliminated. Some desires may be important, but they could be accomplished through specific goals rather than being lifelong pursuits.

Step 4. Narrative. In the desire statement column below, write a description of your desire as if you've already realized it. For instance, use "I will" instead of "I want." It's crucial to write the description first, as it will help you craft the best name for your desire. You may revisit and edit both as the process brings more clarity.

After writing your list, ask yourself: Would I be happy if I lived a life that fulfilled these desires? If I didn't neglect any of them? Could Mark say his life mattered if he lived in faith and dependence on God, was a great husband, a great father with strong relationships with his kids throughout life, enjoyed a healthy and active lifestyle, had the means to be generous with his time, money, and talents to impact others, and had deep, close friendships that lasted until the end? Would that be a good life or what? Your desires may look different, and I hope they are uniquely yours. Let's get to work.

Desire Group	Desire Statement

Step 5. Final Name. In the Desire Column below, determine the final name for each of your lifelong desires, as these will guide your goals for the next 1 to 3 years. Make them count! Choose descriptive names that are memorable and meaningful to you. For example, instead of simply naming a desire "Friends," Mark named his "Deep Friendships," emphasizing quality over quantity. He also elaborated on what this meant in his desire statement—he will do life together with those friends. So, his desire is to have deep, meaningful friendships, with the expectation of spending time with them frequently.

Desire Group	Desire Statement
~~Husband~~ Great Husband	Amy will say that I was a great husband. Loving, caring, wonderful partner, unselfish, and pursued her fiercely until our last days.
~~Father~~ Loving Father	I will have a wonderful relationship with each of my kids, and I will support them and love on them and be there for them when they need me.
~~Friend~~ Deep Friendships	I will have deep friendships to enjoy life with and be there for one another.
~~Physical~~ ~~Active~~ Healthy	I will live a healthy lifestyle, physically fit with a healthy diet as a habit to ensure, God willing, that I can stay active for as long as possible.
~~Giving~~ ~~Serving~~ ~~Volunteer~~ Generous	I will have the means to generously give to others so that I can make an impact in people's lives.
~~Spiritual~~ ~~God~~ ~~Faith~~ God Intimacy	I will have a rich, intimate relationship with God, I will know him and live a life of dependence, in faith, on God.

Recap - Desires

There you have it! Remember, this is a process. If it felt a bit messy, that's completely normal. Hopefully, you now have 3-7 solid desires, and if you live a life that fulfills these desires, you'll be a very happy person who lived a life that mattered.

Concept Review - Goals

The things we want to achieve in life are called goals. We have immediate goals (quarterly), short-term goals (within a year), and long-term goals (over a year).

Goals should be SMART—an acronym that's often mentioned but sometimes needs clarification. SMART stands for Specific, Measurable, Attainable, Relevant, and Timely.

When setting your goals, make sure they are specific. For example, consider the goal of losing weight and how most people set goals versus using the SMART method:

Goal: Lose Weight

Typical Goal Setting:
I'm going to go on a diet and lose some weight!

vs.

SMART Goal Setting:

Specific	I will do the Whole 30 diet in the month of January to lose weight
Measurable	Lose 6 lbs (I currently weigh 195, so my goal is to weigh *under* 190 lbs)
Achievable	Yes! Whole 30 limits alcohol, added sugar, and grains, so I'm bound to meet my goal as I do the diet.
Relevant	Yes! It aligns with my *Healthy* desire.
Timely	Yes, Jan 1 - Jan 31st, and no cheating!

Wow, see the difference? Who do you think is more likely to lose weight—the person who doesn't specify the diet, the actual goal (6 lbs), the timeframe, or connect it to a value or lifetime desire (that we know of)? Or the person who is very specific, has a plan, and not only sets the goal to lose 6 lbs but goes further by defining the goal as being under a certain weight? Why did he do that? Because he's used SMART goal setting before and knows that 6 lbs can be relative to the weight he started with. Did he start at 194...196...195? No, he started at 195, and for him to truly reach his goal, being under 190 is the real target.

He also made his goal relevant by tying it to his lifetime desire to be healthy. Why wouldn't he do this? It just makes sense.

As the saying goes, a goal without a plan is just a dream. SMART goals make your goals real.

Now that we know how to set proper goals, let me blow your mind: The 'R' in SMART has become my favorite part of the acronym. For me, goal setting used to feel random. I wanted to lose weight, save an emergency fund, run a marathon, etc. I also had long-term goals that felt more like desires—own a mountain house, live in Europe for a month every year, etc. Those types of goals seemed more like dreams.

Most of my goals weren't SMART, so I rarely met them, which left me discouraged. Why even set them anymore? Without knowing my lifetime desires to guide my goals, they just felt like random, unachievable dreams.

Well, that's about to change if you're willing to implement this goal-setting method:

Step 1. List your lifetime desires.

Step 2. Write down the ideal or description of what living out that desire ultimately looks like. Remember, as an ideal, this is something to strive towards, not necessarily something to be fully accomplished.

Step 3. Start with your 3 year goal. This gives you a vision of where you are headed. Dream a little here. Bigger than you normally would.

Step 4. Fill in your 1 Year goal. What do you want to accomplish *this year* (in the next 12 months)?

Step 5. Quarterly Goal. What do you need to start doing now to help you meet your 1 year plan?

Setting your goals by time frame and aligning them with your desires can be life-changing. I encourage you to find the willingness to take the time to do this, the courage to dream, and the discipline to achieve your goals. You can thank me for the results later!

So let's look at how this would play out for Mark:

Step 1. Lifetime Desire[13]

Lifetime Desire	Ideal/Desc.	3 Year Goals	1 Year Goals	Quarterly Goals
Loving Father	To have great and active relationships with my kids, loving them as they are and helping without enabling.			

Step 2. Three Year Goal

Lifetime Desire	Ideal/Desc.	3 Year Goals	1 Year Goals	Quarterly Goals
Loving Father	To have great and active relationships with my kids, loving them as they are and helping without enabling.	**Take each kid on a mission trip their senior year.**		

[13] This format is adapted from the Strategic Coach® "Pocket Coach." For more information about Strategic Coach, please visit, www.strategiccoach.com.

Step 3: One Year Goal

Lifetime Desire	Ideal/Desc.	3 Year Goals	1 Year Goals	Quarterly Goals
Loving Father	To have great and active relationships with my kids, loving them as they are and helping without enabling.	Take each kid on a mission trip their senior year.	**Do a regular sport/ game with each child on a monthly basis.**	

Step 4. Quarterly Goal

Lifetime Desire	Ideal/Desc.	3 Year Goals	1 Year Goals	Quarterly Goals
Loving Father	To have great and active relationships with my kids, loving them as they are and helping without enabling.	Take each kid on a mission trip their senior year.	Do a regular sport/game with each child on a monthly basis.	**Take a kid to breakfast once a week.**

That's the process. Please note, if you find a more comfortable order for you to complete the steps, then by all means, do what works for you. I have found what works best for me.

Based on Mark's lifetime desires, here's an example of what his goals would look like:

Lifetime Goal Setting

Lifetime Desire	Ideal/Desc	3 Year Goals	1 Year Goals	Quarterly Goals
Great Husband	Pursued my wife always and to the end.	Do a marriage study/conf. with my wife	Encourage my wife on 3 girl trips by the end of the year	Do date night weekly
Loving Father	Great and active relationships with the kids	Take each kid on a mission trip their senior year	Play a regular sport/game with each child per quarter	Take a kid to breakfast once a week
Healthy	Extremely fit for my age	I weigh my ideal weight	Have healthy diet as a lifestyle	Run the mountain trail race
Deep Friendships	Friends that I can count on and that can count on me.	Start Guys Annual Golfing Trip	Have a regular foursome of 3 guys I really like	Join the Thursday night golf league
Generous	My default is to help people in need, using my resources.	Volunteer 30 days a year	Have a generosity fund, and give $10,000 away per year	Set Up a Donor Advised Fund
God Intimacy	I know God and walk with him daily.	Annual Prayer Retreats	Lead a men's group	Join a men's group at church

FAQ:

How often should you update your goals?

Aim to review and update your goals every quarter. At the end of each year, reassess your 1-year goals and adjust them as needed. This is also a good time to reevaluate your 3-year goals to ensure they still align with your current priorities

Give yourself grace.

Focus on what you've accomplished, not what you haven't. It's okay if a quarterly goal takes two quarters to finish. Progress is progress, and it's worth celebrating. Remember, the goal is to move forward, even if it takes a little longer than expected.

Don't be afraid to change your goals.

Life happens, and priorities shift. It's perfectly fine if your 3-year goals change over time. The key is to keep your goals relevant, adjusting them as circumstances evolve.

SMART goals matter.

Mark's goals are summaries, but each one should ideally be a SMART goal—Specific, Measurable, Achievable, Relevant, and Time-bound. You can refine your summaries to make them more actionable and clear.

Now it's your turn.

Set goals that align with your Lifetime Desires. If you review them regularly and adjust as needed, you'll be amazed at the important and meaningful achievements you'll accomplish.

Lifetime Desire	Ideal/ Desc.	3 Year Goals	1 Year Goals	Quarterly Goals

Recap

To live a life that truly matters, start by identifying your lifetime desires—those core ideals that define what you want your life to stand for. Once you're clear on these desires, use SMART goal setting to progressively turn them into reality.

For these tools and additional resources to develop Manifesto #4 and Manifesto #5, visit www.madetomatter.coach/manifesto.

Manifesto #6: Vision How-To

Concept Review

Vision is the picture of a desired future state. I'm often struck by how little we allow ourselves to truly dream, as if we're tethered to the present and can't imagine a future much different from our current reality. It's understandable. There's a concept I love called cognitive dissonance. When we experience it, we feel discomfort because our brain is trying to reconcile what it believes to be true with the reality it's currently perceiving. So, when you envision a future that's far from your present reality, your brain might resist, causing cognitive discomfort, and urging you to "Stop it! Get back in line!" We often give in to this discomfort, returning to a reality that feels safer and more familiar, allowing us to move on with life more peacefully.

Cognitive Dissonance

There are many things that can cause cognitive dissonance. One major factor is the gap between your actions and your values. For example, if you value honesty but find yourself lying, your brain will struggle with that inconsistency, causing discomfort until you resolve it—either by aligning your actions with honesty or by letting go of that value.

Similarly, if you "talk the talk" but don't "walk the talk," your brain will react negatively. What you say doesn't align with what your brain perceives as reality. Some people learn to live with this discomfort, expending a lot of energy to manage the cognitive dissonance.

A healthier approach is to restore integrity with yourself and your mind. The best way to do this is to live in alignment with who you believe and say you are. In other words, live your values, don't just preach them. Cultivate character by ensuring your actions match your words. Acknowledge your feelings—if your brain knows you're sad but you refuse to cry, that creates dissonance. Address conflicts in your life. If you've offended someone, make amends. If someone has wronged you, address it. Your brain expects harmony in relationships, so unresolved conflict distorts reality. There's wisdom in the saying, "Don't let the sun go down on your anger." Reconcile with your friends, spouse, or children to restore integrity.

Vision Progress > Vision Success

So what does cognitive dissonance have to do with vision? To truly dream, we must give ourselves permission to do so. We need to communicate with our brain, saying, "Hey, we're about to step outside of our current reality and imagine a better future. I need you to let go for a moment and allow me to explore this vision."

It's also important to remind our brain that dreaming doesn't mean we have to achieve the vision 100%. What matters most is making progress toward that vision.

As I mentioned earlier, most people don't dream for two reasons: 1) Cognitive dissonance holds them back, and 2) Fear of failure. They see it as all or nothing—if they dream and don't fully realize that dream, they feel like they've failed. So, they choose not to dream at all.

But you're not most people.

I want you to tell your brain this: "I'm going to dream, and I'm going to dream big. It's okay. We might not achieve the dream exactly as imagined, but just think how incredible it will be if we accomplish even 80% of it! Won't that be amazing?!"

Visualization (the act of picturing your Vision)

It's like a golfer visualizing a 180-yard shot. He imagines a perfectly smooth, tempoed swing, feels the ball explode off his club, and sees himself holding his pose as the ball arcs perfectly toward the pin. It lands five feet in front of the hole, bounces three feet past it, and the backspin pulls it right into the cup! What a shot! Or better yet, what a swing! He can see, feel, and experience that shot in his mind, over and over again. Through practice, he's become skilled at visualization, and it greatly benefits his game.

So, what does he do after picturing this perfect swing? He steps up to the ball, makes a beautiful, tempoed swing, and watches as the ball explodes off his club. He holds his pose, following the ball's climb to its apex and descent toward the pin. The distance is nearly perfect as the ball lands six feet short of the flagstick, takes a bounce, and checks to about three feet left of the hole. The golfer slides his club down through his right hand, like sheathing a sword. What a beautiful shot. He shoulders his golf bag and walks confidently to the green, ready to tap in his birdie putt.

Now, did the golfer fail because he didn't achieve his vision of holing the shot? Absolutely not! His vision helped him execute a remarkable shot. As a golfer, he understands the marksman's adage: "Aim small, miss small." His aim was to hole the shot; his miss left him three feet left, pin high. A beautiful shot!

Vision Exercise

Go ahead, tell your brain that you're going to dream. That you're going to aim small so you only miss small. Close your eyes, take a few deep breaths, and let's dream.

Step 1. Visualize your Desires.

First, I want you to recall the desires you identified in Manifesto #4. Review them and get them clear in your mind's eye. If your desires include deep friendships, great relationships with your kids, and a strong marriage, visualize yourself enjoying time with those people at a ripe old age.

Whatever your desires are, take a moment to visualize them unfolding as you grow older, toward the end of your great life.

Step 2. Dream. Make it Bigger.

With your realized desires clear in your mind, I want you to turn them into a story—and make it big. For Mark, he envisions his desires for his marriage, children, and friendships by picturing himself and his wife in their dream home, spending time playing backyard games with their children, their spouses, and 13 grandchildren at their Italian villa. He imagines golfing with his friends at some of the finest courses... in Ireland.

Step 3. Write it Down.

Once you have that vision crystal clear in your mind's eye, write it down. Remind your brain that it's okay—your brain might judge you and try to pull you back to the present, to the reality it knows. Remember, it's trying to protect you from potential disappointment. But dreaming big and making progress is not a risk; it's success.

Step 4. Vision Statement.

(Optional) Easier said than done, but I encourage you to take your vision and distill it into one sentence. As Abraham Lincoln, Mark Twain, or various others have said: "I would have written you a shorter letter if I had the time." Simplifying and being concise is hard, but give writing a vision statement a shot. Having that statement will serve as a powerful reminder of your overall vision.

Mark's Example Vision Exercise Example:

Step 1. Visualize your Desires.

Great Husband. Amy says that I am a great husband—loving, caring, a wonderful partner, unselfish, and that I pursued her fiercely until our last days. Throughout our marriage, we truly enjoyed being together and supporting each other. Amy wrote her poetry books and published more than she ever imagined. She has great, close friends and meets with them regularly. We play tennis together, travel together, write books together, and do ministry together. We host supper clubs in our dream house. We can't believe that we could fall more in love, but we do—deeper and deeper every day. It's not easy. It takes work and diligence, and I consider it my main job to love my wife. Man, I'm glad I came to that realization 25 years ago!

Loving Father. I have a wonderful relationship with each of my kids. I will support them, love them, and be there when they need me. I can see them as adults, with spouses I also have great relationships with. Each of them has 2 to 3 kids. My children all get along and are closer than I ever imagined! We play golf and tennis together (with their spouses), and we gather twice a year—once for a major holiday and once for a summer trip. My wife and I visit each child at least once a year as well.

Healthy. I live a healthy lifestyle, staying physically fit with a healthy diet as a habit, ensuring, God willing, that I can stay active for as long as possible. I thank God for my health. Toward the end of my life, people marvel at how in shape I am. They say, "You are how old?" I love to walk, ride, and run. Being active is like breathing; it's just a normal part of my day. I love golf and still enjoy beating the young guys on the tennis court. Eating and drinking is a joy because I've learned to do it in moderation. Amy and I have settled into a Mediterranean diet, and we thoroughly enjoy a glass of wine with dinner every night. We've learned that with moderation in both workouts and diet, we can do anything we want as long as we honor that principle. As a result, we feel very free.

Generous. I have the means to give generously to others and make an impact in people's lives. I take great joy in matching whatever contributions my kids make to their kids' 529 plans. Amy and I have adopted an orphanage in Africa, which we visit about every three years. We fully support their staff, which has about a $100,000 per year budget. We've seen thousands of orphans find homes and parents around the world. Because the trip to Africa can be grueling, we bought a villa in Italy to serve as our headquarters when we go. We fly to Italy, stay for a week, then fly to Africa, stay for a week, and return to our villa in Italy for a couple more weeks before heading home. We have also created a kindness fund of $30,000 per year, which we use to help those in need as we become aware of them. Initially, finding people to help was challenging, but as we practiced, we began to see needs everywhere. Each of our children has their own kindness fund too, which they fund and give from.

Deep Friendships. I have deep friendships to enjoy life with and to be there for one another. Both Amy and I have built a wonderful group of friends that we do life with. We host supper clubs, go on golf and tennis outings, do ministry together, work on business ventures, and enjoy shows together. We simply enjoy life with our close friends, and it's a tremendous blessing.

God Intimacy. I have a rich, intimate relationship with God. I will know Him and live a life of dependence, in faith, on God. I could never have imagined being so in love with God. I can't wait to get up in the morning, spend time with Him, read His Word, and talk with Him. I've come to depend on prayer almost like breathing—I'm praying all the time, and I finally understand what "pray without ceasing" means. Amy has grown in the same way with God, and we are completely one with Him as a couple. I have seen God do unbelievable things in my life, and I fully anticipate He will do even more in my final years.

Step 2. Dream. Make it Bigger. (Start from now to you Realizing Your Desires)

Close your eyes. Envision your dream as it unfolds from now until your old age. Like the golfer, see, feel, and sense your life expanding far beyond what you ever imagined possible. You've given your brain permission to dream—now dream!

Step 3. Write it Down.

Mark Dreams Bigger...

I was offered an opportunity that, at the time, I didn't realize would change my life. Life was already pretty good—could it possibly get much better?

My physical therapy practice approached me with an offer to buy into the practice. After much deliberation, Amy and I decided to do so. It turned out to be one of the best decisions I've ever made.

As an owner, I began to see opportunities everywhere. We could improve this and that, and we did. I made new key hires, revamped our scheduling system, and opened another office across town. A couple of years later, I bought out my partners, becoming the sole owner of a two-office practice with 12 physical therapists and 17 employees total. Early on, I made a decision that proved to be fortuitous—I decided to buy the buildings instead of leasing them. So I owned two buildings as well.

At a conference, I met other practice owners who started asking me how to run their practices more efficiently. It struck me that I could charge for this advice, so I began consulting. The consulting practice took off. I hired an assistant to handle scheduling, inquiries, and invoicing. Before long, my time was evenly split between running my own practice and consulting. Soon, I realized I needed to hire someone to manage my practice day-to-day. Fortunately, I was able to promote someone from within, and they thrived as did the practcies. Within five years, I had three locations, bought another building, and grew the staff to nearly 50 employees.

As I consulted more practices, it became clear that they all struggled with similar issues—they were physical therapists, not business owners. I found that if I could get them to hire an operator and focus on their services, their practices would thrive. I also noticed that many didn't own their real estate, and I advised most of them to buy buildings, which many did.

More opportunities came my way as these practices began looking for buyers. The owners were aging out and naturally wanted to sell. I had an idea to form a group and sell it as a nationwide practice to a larger company.

I created a system where I could provide an initial cash buyout, with the owner staying on for a couple of years until we could sell the entire group.

It worked better than I could have ever dreamed. In the end, the group comprised of 18 practices with over 100 locations and 700 employees.

The initial cash outlay to assemble the group was approximately $18,000,000. We sold the group for over $75,000,000, of which I took home $30,000,000. And the real estate was not part of the deal. We now owned 82 locations (not every location owned its building, but most did), and I was the majority owner of that real estate holding, owning more than 30% of a $40,000,000 real estate portfolio.

I was 57, and I wasn't ready to retire. I continued my consulting business but at a fraction of the time I spent before. I assembled another group, much smaller this time—five practices and 15 locations, all in one state. We sold that group for $9,000,000 and added 11 more locations to our real estate portfolio.

At the age of 63, I was fully "retired" but busier than ever. With well into the eight figures in the bank and a residual income from the real estate, I certainly didn't need to work anymore.

And I did something I thought I'd never do—I bought into fractional ownership of a jet. I always thought there would be no way I could afford a jet, and even if I had the income, I'd never own one. I remember when paying $400 for a fancy golf round seemed expensive, but not a big deal. Now, paying thousands in jet fuel per hour isn't that big of a deal. The freedom a jet provides is a luxury I could never have imagined.

Thankfully, I've never been into boating or fishing, so I'm not flushing any of my hard-earned money down the toilet on those hobbies!

During this journey, my wife and I built a marriage ministry, as marriage was one of our passions, and we wanted to see couples succeed. We wrote a book together and spoke often at conferences. We saw thousands of marriages restored through our book and speaking. But an even greater impact was that Amy wrote a marriage curriculum used by churches around the world. God used us to impact tens of thousands of marriages.

We finally bought our dream house at the age of 52. It's a stone house, just like the one at Capital City Club in Atlanta. It looks like it came out of a Thomas Kinkade painting (sans the obnoxious light shinig from within!). It has a rounded front door with fluted glass. People love our house and often drive by slowly, taking pictures. It sits on two acres and has a yard to die for. Thankfully, I don't have to maintain it—Amy and a yard service company take care of it. It's not huge by most standards, but then again, it is by the world's standards. At 3,700 square feet, it has a nice master bedroom, two ensuite bedrooms, and an additional guest bedroom. There's a theater and a cold bunk room for the grandkids. We have our own workout room with a Peloton, full weight set, treadmill, and ample space for yoga and other workouts. I did splurge on my own golf simulator, which is unbelievably realistic. It's pretty fun to play Pebble Beach on a Tuesday evening.

My favorite part of the house is the outdoor living space. Amy finally got her pool. Right off the great room, bi-fold patio doors fold open to a teak dining table, an outdoor kitchen, and off to the side, games galore—horseshoes, bocce ball, cornhole, a stone ping pong table, and more. It's designed for our adult children and grandchildren, and we love having them over.

Two of our kids live in Greenville, so we see them often. They, of course, love the pool and come over to use it. One of our kids lives out of town, but makes annual visits and we visit them as well. We usually get together for Thanksgiving or Christmas and let them decide where. Usually, they pick our home.

I often escape to the mountains to my off-grid cabin. Inspired by Sundance, Robert Redford's place in Utah, I bought a rustic compound and kept it that way. The goal was simplicity. I wanted to leave all the comforts of life in the city and enjoy the mountains. So there's nothing fancy—no granite countertops, no rain shower heads, or white marble anywhere. Just timber, a tin roof, wood planks, and simple furniture.

Like home, there are games galore, but no electronics—no phones, TVs, or anything. You can only eat, drink, read, play games, write, and talk. I did splurge by making it 100% sustainable. It has solar power, battery storage, and a rainwater cistern supplemented by a well. We entertain friends there, and they are always blown away by how refreshed they feel after a long weekend with us. We also use the compound for our marriage ministry and let churches and other groups host retreats there.

I also bought a place in the Bahamas and one out West. My kids use both places more than we do, which is great. We also offer the properties, like the mountain compound, as places of refreshment for ministry and friends.

The last of my material possession updates is the villa in Italy. I'm almost embarrassed to say I own five properties. I never thought I'd want the hassle. However, I don't hassle with it much since I have a family office that handles the properties and investments. Does that sound arrogant? When you don't have the money, it can seem that way, I get it. But when you do have the money, you want the time to enjoy it! So I do, and I pay people who gladly take care of the properties and other details in life.

Back to the villa—it's a seven-bedroom villa with a bunk room, guest house, great Tuscan views, a wonderful chef's kitchen, a pool, an olive grove, and a small vineyard. We have a caretaker and a groundskeeper. There's a Mercedes van for shuttling people around, a convertible MG, and a BMW. We always wanted a place in Europe, and our Italian villa is a dream come true.

We also use the villa pragmatically. We support several schools and orphanages in Africa. Traveling to and from Africa from the United States can be a grueling 30-hour trip (the jet can't make that trip, unfortunately!). So we use the villa as our headquarters—flying into

Florence, staying a week at the villa, then flying down to Uganda, spending time at the orphanage, and returning to Italy for a week or two before heading back to the States. It's a beautiful strategy, in my opinion. We also have others from the States use the villa for similar purposes.

The orphanages have placed thousands of children in homes around the world, bringing indescribable joy to my wife and me. I've also funded an African business training organization and volunteer my time mentoring African businesspeople.

Any parent's dream is for their children to be happy. I can't say it's been smooth sailing—life doesn't work that way. But I can say my children are happy. They have healthy marriages that they work diligently to nurture. They're raising great children, whom we enjoy spoiling. We also enjoy watching the grandkids torment their parents by doing the same things they used to do to us (we warned them that payback would be hell).

My biggest concern is that my wealth might corrupt my kids and even my grandchildren in some way. It's a tightrope I walk—offering luxuries and respites to my children that most people don't have the opportunity to enjoy, while also ensuring there are no handouts. They have to earn their way, though there are things I'm doing that they don't know about that I hope will be helpful later. My father gave me a great gift—no school debt and a used car when I graduated. I've done the same for my kids. If their spouses had school debt, I helped eliminate it quicker by matching whatever they were paying. Lastly, I matched their 529 college savings for their kids. I want to spoil my grown kids, but I know they have to earn their own way, too. So I spoil them a little and let them earn the rest on their own.

I'm still a single-digit handicap golfer and will be into my early 70s.

Tennis is a joy, and I play twice a week. Trips with friends, hosting people at our house, doing couples' ministry, and spending time with our kids keep us busier than ever. I've written seven books now, three of which are bestsellers. One is on sex in marriage (co-written with my wife), another bestseller is *How to Roll Forward an Empire* (my story of building and selling the physical therapy practices), and *The Life that Matters Manifesto*. My favorite book, which didn't make it as a bestseller but probably has changed more lives than my other books. The one book I hand out most is *The Only Thing You Need*, which is my story of how I finally learned to be 100% dependent on God.

I never thought being a "super Christian" would be me. I always thought I'd have a normal spiritual life, but I find myself with an immensely rich relationship with God. I can't get enough of the Bible. I can't stop praying, and I'm now that guy who talks about Him all the time. He's been so good to me—not only with money and material things, but with relationships—my wife, my kids, their spouses, my grandchildren, my friends, business partners, ministry partners, and more. When people say their cup overflows, I thought I knew what they meant, but I had no idea! God has used me in ways I could never have comprehended before. Only God could do this. Now my days start with Him, are 100% dependent on Him, and I trust Him completely. I do the things He tells me to do. There are often days when I cancel everything because He wants me to do something else, and I'm totally fine with that. I get to see God bless so many people and touch so many lives, and it has nothing to do with me and everything to do with what God does through me. It's quite remarkable.

I could go on and on. But to wrap this up, there's one thing that Amy and I enjoy almost more than anything else. I remember watching *Brewster's Millions* as a kid, a movie about a guy (played by Richard Pryor) who had to give away $30,000,000 in a month. He thought it would be easy. He discovered how hard it was to spend $1,000,000 a day.

I've always wanted to cultivate the gift and habit of being generous. So we've set a goal to give $1,000,000 away a year—but not by writing checks to charities. Actually giving—handing people—a million dollars in cash throughout the year. You think that's easy? Do the math. That's $2,800 a day.

Every morning, I come to the kitchen, and there are two stacks of fourteen $100 bills. A sticky note on them says, "God will show you who needs this today."

Sure enough, on my way to play golf, there's a car on the side of the road with a mom and three kids. I pull over, help change a tire, and see the need. I hand her all fourteen $100 bills in an envelope and say God was thinking about her today and every day. Then I pull away before she can hand it back, as I've discovered most people do. Most people are too proud to accept charity. Little do they know it's not charity—it's grace, a gift from God that they don't deserve, but God gives it to them anyway because He loves them. I'm just the messenger, the delivery boy.

The next day, I'm in line at the grocery store, and an elderly woman is trying to check out. Her card is declined. She's flabbergasted and about to leave all her groceries and walk away. I discreetly catch the cashier's attention and signal that I'll pay for her groceries. As we walk out of the store, I catch up with the woman and hand her an envelope. "Someone wanted you to have this," I say, smile, and keep walking. I sensed God didn't want me to give her all the money, so I gave her $1,000. I didn't know why at the time.

Later, I drop by the drug store, and in the parking lot, there's a lady crying. I ask her if everything's okay. She says no, it's not. She needed to get her dad a prescription that his insurance no longer covers, and she can't afford it. I ask her how much it is. She says $400. I smile, reach into my pocket, and hand her the $400 that I knew was waiting for her.

And that... is just two days. My wife and I sit down every night with a glass of wine and exchange stories of how God worked that day and how He led us to those in need. They were there all along—it's just that our eyes are now opened.

At the end of my life, I look back and recognize that I had such a full life. I was fulfilled. My cup overflowed. God was so good to me. There was absolutely no sorrow in heading home. I had my fill on earth, and I was ready for eternity with Him.

Step 4. Vision Statement.

Through an intimate relationship with God, I kept my eyes open to what he was doing, joined him without hesitation in both trust and faith in order to help people, and lived a life beyond my imagination, enjoying marriage, relationships, success, wealth, God, and a life to the fullest.

Review

Wow. I didn't know Mark's life would turn out like that! Incredible! Almost ridiculous, right? But that's the point. Make your vision ridiculous. Suspend your "Now." It's your turn. My challenge to you is to dream bigger than you've ever dreamed. Spend some time on this. Invest in yourself. Dream big!

Step 1. Visualize your Desires. Get your list of desires, and like the golfer, close your eyes and visualize those desires becoming a reality.

Step 2. Dream. Make it Bigger. Now, allow yourself to get a little ridiculous and dream big. Tell your brain it's okay—you're just trying something new, so there's no need to freak out. Close your eyes again, and imagine how your life will unfold from now until your passing in old age.

Step 3. Write it Down. Once you've dreamed big, write it all down without judgment. Resist the urge to hold back or play it safe. Let yourself go and capture every idea freely!

Step 4. Vision Statement. After writing your dream-big vision, distill its essence into a concise vision statement. Include this in your Life that Matters Manifesto.

Recap

Remember, when you can see it, know it, and say it, your brain begins to believe it as your new reality. As it becomes your reality, you'll start to notice opportunities arising, almost as if you're manifesting your vision—and in a way, you are. What's happening is that you've given your brain permission to accept your vision as true, which drives your actions to achieve more desirable results.

There's tremendous upside to visualization, and I sincerely hope you'll invest the time and energy in yourself to create a compelling, bigger-than-you-can-imagine vision for your future. Good luck!

For these tools and additional resources to develop Manifesto #6, visit www.madetomatter.coach/manifesto.

Manifesto #7: Mission Exercise

Concept Review

Your mission is a 1-5 year objective that serves as the bridge connecting your purpose to your vision. With your purpose and vision as your bookends, it's time to determine the mission you are on. Other factors influencing your mission include, but are not limited to:

- Current Life Circumstances
- Your Desires and Goals
- Your Passions
- And basically all of the other Life that Matters criteria such as Causes, Higher Calling, Values, etc.

For Mark, his purpose is: To help people who want to be better.

His vision is: Through an intimate relationship with God, I kept my eyes open to what he was doing, joined him without hesitation in both trust and faith in order to help people, and lived a life beyond my imagination, enjoying marriage, relationships, success, wealth, God, and a life to the fullest.

Mark's Current Circumstances:

He's a Physical Therapist, married, has 3 kids or 4?

What would Mark's current mission be, based on all these factors? He wants to help those who seek help. His vision is to live life to the fullest while helping others do the same. He's diligently preparing to afford college for his kids, which is fast approaching. He loves his profession and feels privileged to mentor other physical therapists. Additionally, he and his wife are involved in marriage ministry. Mark is living very intentionally.

However, Mark senses that he doesn't want to be a physical therapist forever—at least not as the one providing the service. He desires a broader influence and to help more people. While he doesn't yet know what that will look like, he trusts it's part of God's plan.

One morning, he sits down to reflect on his mission. He reviews his purpose and vision, and determines that his mission for the next 3-5 years is to transition out of direct PT service and move into teaching or a role where he can have a greater impact.

Mark's Mission:

Transition from the day-to-day practice of PT to Administration/Operations or Teaching to have a bigger impact helping people in 3-5 years.

Now, guess what? With Mark's purpose, mission, and vision aligned, what do you think will happen? That's right—his goals will begin to align as well. His actions, perceptions, and reality will start to shift, and he'll begin noticing and "manifesting" opportunities.

Almost subconsciously, after defining his mission, Mark began paying closer attention to how the practice was running. He started considering how he could improve things and what changes he would make if he had more responsibility. Little did he know, the owner was contemplating selling the practice. The owner also noticed Mark's increased engagement and knew Mark had a good head on his shoulders and a stable life. "Maybe, just maybe... Mark would be interested in buying," the owner thought.

Your Mission:

Step 1. Review your purpose and your vision. Write them below.

Purpose Assessment:

Purpose Statement:

Vision Statement:

Step 2. Visualize. Based on your purpose and vision, where do you see yourself in three to five years? Recall the visualization principles from the vision chapter. Allow your mind to dream freely.

3-5 Years Visualization:

Step 3. Mission Statement. Using the SMART Goal framework (Specific, Measurable, Attainable, Relevant, and Timely), write your 3-5 year goal to accomplish the vision you visualized above.

Mission Statement:

Congratulations! Let your mission statement sink in and record it on the Life that Matters Manifesto.

Recap

Your mission is the bridge that connects your purpose and vision. Using visualization and the SMART goal-setting concept, determine your mission that will help you achieve your vision.

###

For these tools and additional resources to develop Manifesto #7, visit www.madetomatter.coach/manifesto.

Manifesto #8: Your Super-Genius How-To

Concept Review:

You have a Super-Genius, which is a set of talents that, when combined, allows you to do what you do better than most people. When you own your Super-Genius, you become even more unique in what you do.

Super-Genius Exercise:

There are three exercises we'll do to hone in on your Super-Genius. Remember, I think you already know what it is. However, it's been my experience that even though the answer is right there in front of you, it can be awfully difficult for you to see the reality about yourself. So if you find yourself spinning your wheels to figure out what your Super-Genius is, stop. Instead, I want you to use two of the exercises below to get outside, objective input that will give you the answers you are seeking.

Step 1. Take the CliftonStrengths° Assessment. This is one of the best assessments I've seen on Super-Genius. Of the 34 strengths that make up the model, the assessment will rank all 34, but it encourages you to concentrate on the top 5. Those are your key strengths.

Goto: www.madetomatter.coach/clifton5 to take the assessment. Please note, at the time of this publishing, it costs ~$25, and it's worth every penny. If you want the full report that gives you all 34 themes, the cost is ~$50 and can be accessed at www.madetomatter.coach/clifton34.

Record Your Top 5 Strengths (and their overview) here:

1.

2.

3.

4.

5.

Step 2. Get Super-Genius Feedback from those close to you. Send your Super-Genius letter to your peers, friends, and family, asking them for their feedback. I recommend you email them the following letter (feel free to edit as you think necessary) and be specific about when you need it back (otherwise, it's unlikely you will get it back!).

Tom,

I'm reading a book called Live a Life that Matters, and one of the chapters is to ask those who know me well to give me some insight around my unique strengths. I'd really appreciate it if you could provide me some feedback on the following:

- *What do you think I'm best at?*
- *What skills or abilities do you think comes most naturally to me?*
- *What traits or characteristics do you think I exhibit as strengths?*
- *When's a time you've experienced me at my best and why?*

Thank you for your feedback and taking the time to respond. I'd really appreciate it if you could do so by next Friday at 5pm. I plan to spend a day that weekend to pull the responses together to get a better understanding of my strengths.

-Mark

###

Stop. Don't run away! Many people resist this step (I procrastinated for two years before I finally sent my letters!). This seems a little self-serving, and it is. Remember that I asked you to give yourself permission to be selfish? **The responses you get from people will be some of the most cherished letters you'll ever receive.** When I did this, I was blown away by people's responses—the time they took, the insight they had, the things that came up that I had no idea about myself, and the themes from many of the respondents that cropped up. This exercise is really priceless.

Don't run from it. Do it. You'll be blessed, I promise.

Step 3. Summarize the Responses. Once you've received all of your responses, go through them and circle the keywords, phrases, and ideas in each letter. Review all of the letters and find the patterns. What keeps coming up? What things are being said differently but are really the same idea? For instance, here are some of the patterns Mark found:

You're an incredible teacher.
You always take the time to help. You really care.
You have a natural knack for business that you underestimate.

All of these are pointing to Mark's Super-Genius: As a business leader in a business that provides care.

Once you have gone through your responses, record your top 5-10
strengths + attributes here:

1.   6.

2.   7.

3.   8.

4.   9.

5.   10.

Step 4. Pull it all together into your Super-Genius Statement

Using the CliftonStrengths™ assessment and your Super-Genius
Letter Responses, I want you to create a description of your Super-
Genius that you would use to describe yourself to someone who asks.
Use the following framework:

My Super-Genius is a culmination of the following superpowers:

_____,
(superpower 1)

_____, _____, that I use to
(superpower 2)   (superpower 3)

_____.
    (those I help / result / impact)

Example 1:

My Super-Genius is a culmination of the following super-powers:

<u>I can fly,</u>
(superpower 1)

<u>I'm super strong,</u> <u>I'm practically invincible,</u> and
(superpower 2)   (superpower 3)

<u>I have x-ray vision</u> that I use to
(superpower 4)

<u>Help victims who can't help themselves. Ok, basically save the world.</u>
    (those I help / result / impact)

Example 2:

My Super-Genius is a culmination of the following super-powers:

<u>I can crawl up walls,</u>
    (superpower 1)

I can shoot webbing from my wrists,
   (superpower 2)

that allows me to swing through the city, or wrap-up bad guys, and
   (superpower 3)

I have special warning sense that keeps me out of danger.
   (superpower 4)

that I use all of these to
Help victims who can't help themselves. Ok, basically save the world.
   (those I help / result / impact)

You're Turn, Let's try it again:

My Super-Genius is a culmination of the following super-powers:

_____,
   (superpower 1)

_____, _____, that I use to
   (superpower 2)   (superpower 3)

_____.
   (those I help / result / impact)

And if you want to have a little fun with it, based on what you wrote,
your superhero name is:

Superhero Name

Wrapping it up. Let's look at Mark's example:

Step 1. Clifton Strengths[14]:

1. **Maximizer**
   People exceptionally talented in the Maximizer theme focus on strengths as a way to stimulate personal and group excellence. They seek to transform something strong into something superb.

2. **Restorative**
   People exceptionally talented in the Restorative theme are adept at dealing with problems. They are good at figuring out what is wrong and resolving it.

3. **Achiever**
   People exceptionally talented in the Achiever theme work hard and possess a great deal of stamina. They take immense satisfaction in being busy and productive.

4. **Empathy**
   People exceptionally talented in the Empathy theme can sense other people's feelings by imagining themselves in others' lives or situations.

5. **Positivity**
   People exceptionally talented in the Positivity theme have contagious enthusiasm. They are upbeat and can get others excited about what they are going to do.

---

[14] CliftonStrengths' Theme descriptions from https://www.gallup.com/cliftonstrengths/

Step 2 + 3. Summarize the Super-Genius Letter Responses

1. Loving	*6. Listener*
2. Teacher	*7. Excellence*
3. Healer	*8. Optimistic / Positive*
4. Next-Level Pusher	*9. Big Picture*
5. Purpose-Driven	*10. Faith*

Step 4. Super-Genius Statement

My Super-Genius is a culmination of the following superpowers: <u>to care</u>
<u>*for and help others,*</u>
(superpower 1)

<u>*Teach them new skills and abilities,*</u>
        (superpower 2)

<u>*and do so with purpose and excellence,*</u> *that I use to*
        (superpower 3)

<u>*To help them maximize their lives.*</u>
(those I help / result / impact)

Step 5. Superhero Name:

Professor Next-Level

Summary

Your Super-Genius is the culmination of your superpowers. Superman doesn't try to climb walls. Spider-Man doesn't try to fly. They use their Super-Genius to fulfill their purpose, their mission. It would be crazy for them not to use their superpowers.

Embrace your gifts. Write your CliftonStrengths™ on the Life that Matters Manifesto, along with your Super-Genius Letter summarized responses, your Super-Genius Statement, and your Superhero Name, if you chose to do that part of the exercise!

Recap

Your Super-Genius is the unique combination of your superpowers. Yes, you have them. And yes, those close to you can tell you what they are. Discover them. Know them. Own them, as they will help you live a Life that Matters.

For these tools and additional resources to develop Manifesto #8, visit www.madetomatter.coach/manifesto.

Manifesto #9: Vocational Alignment How-To

Concept Review:

According to a 2020 Gallup® poll, only 38% of Americans are engaged in their work. "Engaged" means they are enthusiastic and committed to their work and their workplace.[15] However, that also means that 62% of working Americans are NOT engaged in the workplace. They are not enthusiastic nor committed to their work. For them, we can deduce that work is just a necessary evil, simply a job that one has to do to earn a living. "Grin and bear it" seems to be the code most workers live by.

That's sad. As previously mentioned, we're at work more during our waking hours than we are at home (assuming you work on-premise). Work is a big part of our lives, and we have a choice: we can either see work as just a job, or we can view it as an extension of ourselves. In the latter case, it can be a place where we use our talents, express ourselves, make a contribution, be part of a team, serve others, champoin a cause, and even live out our higher calling.

But a super-majority of Americans don't see it that way, don't try to, or don't believe work can be such a place.

Aligning your vocation with your purpose and the rest of the Life that Matters hierarchy is a fabulous opportunity to make your life

---

[15] https://www.gallup.com/workplace/313313/historic-drop-employee-engagement-follows-record-rise.aspx

157

matter more. Imagine going to work and being fulfilled every day. Imagine waking up on Monday morning excited to go to work. Imagine customers and your boss thanking and appreciating you for the incredible work you do and the contributions you make.

However, I also want to bring some balance to this. Work is work. There's a level of entitlement among some people who believe the universe should provide them with a job they love in every way. But no, you are not entitled! Only recently, historically speaking, have you had the privilege to choose the type of work or company that suits you best. Moreover, it is within your ability to go and try to secure that work. Yet, let's make no mistake about it: work is work. It's meant to be hard. It's meant to be a challenge. There will be some parts of your job you don't enjoy doing, or that may not be the perfect fit for your skills and passions. Still, the more you can align your work—though it likely won't be 100%—with your Life that Matters Manifesto, you will be in the top 38% club as someone who is enthusiastic and committed to their work.

So how do we do this? How do we find the job or career that aligns with our purpose, talents, and vision while meeting our needs such as income, lifestyle, and more? Check out the exercise that follows.

Vocation Alignment Exercise:

How much money would you invest to have the perfect job? Seriously, how much? $1,000? $10,000? More? Once you have that number in your head, I want you to think about investing that much time (based on your hourly rate) in this exercise. Yes, this exercise is a bit involved. I could have made it simpler, but I believe it's so important that the steps are absolutely worth it! Here's what I suggest: read through the steps, review the example, *and then go back and read through the steps again.*

Step 1. Review your Purpose, Passions and Clifton StrengthFinders. List your purpose below as well as your top 5 Clifton Strengths.

Purpose:

Top 5 Clifton Strengths:

Top 5 Super-Genius:

Top 5 Passions:

Step 2. Get Context.

On a scale of 1-10, consider your current job with respect to your purpose, passions, and strengths (see table). Rank each of the following attributes above, with 10 being totally aligned and 1 being not part of the job at all. For instance, in the category of income potential, 10 is outstanding, and 1 is pathetic.

Add up the total scores of the attributes you rank (i.e., the total of your purpose, passions, strengths, super genius, and income) and divide by that total number (in the example, you would divide by 17) to get the average. Pro Tip: Add up each section and then add those totals to get the final sum. In math terms, this is called "chunking."

Step 3. Good, Better, Best.

Based on your purpose and other criteria, think of three jobs that would be improvements over your current job (or company). It could be in a different industry. It could be at a different level (like manager, director, or vice president). It could involve becoming an entrepreneur or joining a startup. Or, if you're a teacher, maybe it's moving into administration. If you're an employee-producer, it could mean moving into management. Your options are limitless and could include changing industries, roles, levels, and many more opportunities.

Whatever your three new options are, rank each according to the criteria, then total and average the scores. Once you've calculated the averages, update the heading at the top so Good / Better / Best is accurate. Sometimes you may find that your current position is the best, which can be great information to have!

Step 4. Gap Analysis.

What do you have to do to get from where you currently are to the best, most optimized vocation? For instance, if your current job is as an employee-producer, and your ideal job would be as the director of that department (i.e., you love your company and your department), you may deduce the following:

1. Understand the Promotion Path
2. Understand the skills needed for that path
3. Speak to my manager/HR to put a plan in place to develop skills
4. Brainstorm about going above and beyond my current responsibilities
5. Set a goal to become the director in 5 years.

Mark's Example

	Current	Good	Better	Best
Job	Physical Therapist	PT Practitioner and Teacher	PT Practice Manager	PT Practice Owner
Description	Provide PT Services as a practitioner	Do both PT and Teach on the side as well	Oversee PT's, and the Office	Own the Practice
Purpose: To help people be better that want to be helped	8	10	10	10
Strengths:	44	47	48	50
1. Maximizer	8	9	9	10
2. Restorative	10	10	10	10
3. Achiever	7	8	9	10
4. Empathy	10	10	10	10
5. Positivity	9	10	10	10

Super-Genius	38	46	50	50
1. Care-Help	9	10	10	10
2. Teach	7	10	10	10
3. Excellence	8	9	10	10
4. Impact	7	8	10	10
5. Maximize	7	9	10	10
Top 5 Passions	38	46	43	49
1 Faith	7	8	9	10
2 Teach	7	9	9	9
3 Help	10	10	9	10
4 Adventure	7	7	8	10
5 Marriage	8	8	8	10
Income Potential	7	6	8	10
Total	135	155	159	169
Average (17 items)	7.94	9.12	9.35	9.94

Your Turn:

	Current	Good	Better	Best
Job				
Description				
Purpose:				
Strengths:				
1.				
2.				
3.				
4.				
5.				
Super-Genius				
1.				
2.				
3.				
4.				
5.				
Top 5 Passions				
1				
2				
3				
4				
5				

Income Potential				
Total				
Average (16)				

With this exercise, Mark realized that what he was doing was already quite good. If he supplemented it with teaching, his income might actually decrease. Although teaching would provide him with more job satisfaction, it didn't align as closely with his vision. When he transitioned into management, both his income and autonomy increased, giving him more time for his marriage, family, and the adventures they loved. When he considered owning his own practice, his "Life that Matters" criteria lit up like a Christmas tree. This path would allow him to use his gifts—caring, helping, teaching, and purpose-driven actions—not only to maximize results for himself and his family but also for his clients and employees.

Step 4. Mark's Gap Analysis

Mark was a good PT with teaching abilities and a natural talent for leadership, though he wasn't formally trained as a leader. He had little to no management experience and had never dealt with financials beyond his home finances. That alone would have scared most people away from trying to change their circumstances—but not Mark. He's an achiever, so he put a plan together:

1. **Get familiar with what it takes to run a practice.** Mark had a friend who owned a Physical Therapy practice in a neighboring state. Mark was going to take a week off and shadow his friend to see how operations ran.

2. **Understand the General Manager role.** Mark figured he had two options (but probably more). He could get paid to learn how to manage a practice, or go start one himself. Based

on his circumstances in life, he liked the less risky route of staying put. When he visited his friend's practice, he would pick the brain of the general manager to understand her job.

3. **Take Management Courses.** Mark would approach his practice owner to see if he could take management courses and express interest in being a manager one day.

4. **Be Proactive.** He would take what he learned and start improving the practice with small, but noticeable changes. Something that would keep him in his lane, but get the attention of management that Mark was a team player.

5. **Take on More Responsibility.** With the previous four steps completed, he would approach the General Manager to express his interest in a larger role, ask how he could contribute, and offer specific recommendations for ways he could be helpful.

6. **Develop.** He would get his hands on every management, leadership, and business book he could find, committing to read at least one per quarter.

Wow. Nice plan! What, did you think Mark was joking around? No, once he completed the Vocational Alignment Grid, he was convinced that owning his own practice would be one of his biggest and most rewarding endeavors ever. It became his number one objective, his mission, and if you know Mark, you know he was going to make it happen.

Now, go make it happen. Update your Life that Matters Manifesto with the aligned target vocation of your choosing.

Review

Aligning your vocation with your Life that Matters Manifesto criteria could be one of the most rewarding things you ever do. If you've already achieved that, congratulations! You're not only in the top 38% but likely in the top 1% of people worldwide who have a job they love and find fulfilling. Remember, having that is not an entitlement; it's a privilege. The world isn't going to hand it to you on a silver platter. You'll probably need to put in some work and take some risks to make it happen. But it will be so worth it!

###

For these tools and additional resources to develop Manifesto #9, visit www.madetomatter.coach/manifesto.

Manifesto #10 and #11: Higher Living How-To

As you journey to Live a Life that Matters, you've discovered your purpose, values, passions, desires, Super-Genius, vocational alignment, and a vision for your life.

That's a lot—and it's all about how you're going to impact those around you. But if you want to put your life into hyperdrive, using all of your unique qualities to serve a cause or higher calling will make your life matter even more.

Concept Review - Causes

A cause is a movement for societal change that is bigger than you. Joining a cause means putting some skin in the game. It's more than just being passionate or ranting on social media about your beliefs; it's about giving of your resources, like your time, talents, and money.

Exercise-Causes

There are numerous websites like https://engage.pointsoflight.org/ that can help you find causes both locally and topically. You can search by keywords to find causes, organizations, and opportunities you're passionate about. Once you've identified a cause of interest, you can volunteer and get involved. If adopting a cause feels like the right step to enhance your Life that Matters, follow these steps:

Step 1. Determine How You Would Like to Get Involved.

Do you want to volunteer, donate, or do both? Would you like to offer services pro bono? How much time can you commit to the cause? Is one night a week for two hours enough, or are you considering volunteering a day or a week each year? Be clear about what you're willing to commit.

Step 2. Understand Your Passions before the Cause.

What are you passionate about? Who do you want to help? For example, Mark loves teaching and physical therapy. He knows new graduates struggle to start their careers. He also values marriage and is passionate about helping couples thrive and avoid divorce. Finally, he has a heart for one of the most vulnerable groups: orphans. These are all causes he wants to support, and he has identified his passions and the areas where he wants to make a difference. Now, he needs to find the right organizations to partner with to have an impact.

Step 3. Find the Organization based on your passions.

Using sites like Points of Light, search for causes and organizations that align with your passions. If you're unsure which specific causes you want to support, identify three that align with your Life that Matters Manifesto.

Step 4. Contact the Organization

Reach out to the organization to learn about their needs and the level of commitment they require. Determine how well this aligns with your Life that Matters Manifesto and the time you have available to serve.

Organization/ Cause:	Example 1	Example 2	Example 3
Passions			
1.	Y / N	Y / N	Y / N
2.	Y / N	Y / N	Y / N
3.	Y / N	Y / N	Y / N
4.	Y / N	Y / N	Y / N
5.	Y / N	Y / N	Y / N
Time Commitment			
Time Available			
Rank (1, 2, 3)			

Mark's Example:

Organization/ Cause:	PT School	Marriage Ministry	Africa Orphanage
Passions			
1 Faith	N	Y	Y
2 Teach	Y	Y	N
3 Help	Y	Y	Y
4 Adventure	N	Y	Y
5 Marriage	N	Y	Y
Time Commitment	90 minutes a week	2 hours a week	2 weeks a year
Time Available	3 hours a week		
Impact (Scale of 1-10)	7	9	10
Rank (A, B, C)	C	A	B

For Mark, there isn't a bad choice, but the grid helped him realize that, given his current circumstances, the Marriage Ministry would be the best use of his time. While the Orphanage has incredible impact potential, it requires a larger commitment in both time and money. Although he would love to teach physical therapy, the grid revealed that this option doesn't have as significant an impact and doesn't involve his wife and family. To satisfy his passion for teaching, he'll focus on mentoring new employees in his practice. However, the best choice for his current situation is the Marriage Ministry.

Keep in mind that the grids used in this book are flexible. If there are other criteria from your Life that Matters Manifesto that you want to consider when choosing a cause, feel free to include them! The grid is simply a tool to help you think through and evaluate what's most important to you.

Recap - Causes

Finding a cause that aligns with your Life that Matters is similar to the challenge of finding a vocation that fits. But the effort will be worth it. There's something magical about serving a cause bigger than yourself. The impact you help create will be incredibly rewarding. Like with all the exercises, I encourage you to commit to finding the right cause by investing the time and thought needed to do so!

Concept Review - Higher Calling

I will first start by saying that telling you "how to" get a higher calling in your life is beyond the scope of this book! However, like a cause, having a higher calling is living a Life that Matters on steroids. A higher calling requires believing in a higher power. And when you believe in that higher power, you feel that you have a purpose, vision, and a connected mission that makes up your higher calling.

Exercise - Higher Calling

Let's delve into how you might gain a higher calling or enhance a calling you may already have. Note that I am going to speak from a Judeo-Christian perspective because I am more familiar with that, and I do not know the nuances of other religions. If you believe in another religion, feel free to substitute and adapt your beliefs to what I'm saying to make it relevant to you.

Step 1. Believe in a Higher Power.

Believing in a higher power means having faith in something greater than yourself. Faith involves believing in the "unseen." If you don't have a higher power to believe in but want to, then what higher power will you choose? You might look back to your childhood to determine if that's a higher power you want to believe in or not. For me, I wouldn't have had much to go on other than that my parents occasionally took us to an Episcopalian church. So I would start there. I'd find an Episcopal church in town, attend some Eucharists, begin to ask questions, and decide if that's the faith I want to follow.

I know, it sounds like I'm simplifying religion, and I am. I think a lot of people make it this really big, personal issue, when it really boils down to: "Are you going to believe in God or not? Or, are you going to play God instead?" God is God. He's put the offer out there, and it's up to you if you're willing to accept it. Again, that sounds simplistic, but I'll remind you that telling you how to believe in God is not within the scope of this book. However, I do believe the question comes down to whether you believe God is really God. If that answer is yes...Then. Just. Believe.

Step 2. Pray for Your Calling.

Once you believe in a higher being, begin to ask God (the higher power) to reveal His will, and then ask Him to show you what He wants you to get involved in. I'd encourage you to be patient. God's timing is not man's timing. But if you live in faith and trust in Him, He will reveal a calling to you.

Step 3. Depend and Trust.

As if steps 1 and 2 weren't hard enough! Maybe this is why so few people live out a higher calling! Trust your Higher Power to lead the way. Keep your eyes open for what He is doing, and when you see Him act, join Him! To the best of your ability, trust God to take care of you. Be dependent on Him, and trust that He will provide what you need. You still need to be responsible, but at the same time, avoid forcing things to happen. He will make things happen. You just need to be willing to go with the flow.

There's nothing more exhilarating than when your life is aligned with God's plan. He tells us that man plans his path, but the Lord determines his steps. Your Life that Matters Manifesto is your path. Daily dependence and trust in Him let Him determine your steps.

Some people I know of who have answered higher callings include Mother Teresa, who dedicated her entire life to orphans in India. I have friends in Atlanta who are on a mission to lead businessmen to Christ. A person in Greenville, SC, is devoted to rolling out a marriage ministry to married couples. Another man and his wife have given their lives to help underprivileged children. A man who is devoted to building homes for the homeless as an example of Christ's love. Couples who believe their home is God's home and open their homes and lives to be foster parents. And businesspeople who believe the same about their businesses, throwing the doors wide open and asking God to do what He wants through their business. That has resulted in amazing cultures where employees are loved on and thrive like in no other business. As previously stated: those I know who are maximizing their lives to matter have a higher calling.

A higher calling does not mean you are going to Africa (though Africa is cool). It doesn't mean you're going to become a preacher. It does mean that you trust and love your God so much that you'd be willing to do what He asks of you. That you would let Him direct your steps. And that's why so few people have a higher calling. They want to be their own God, and that just doesn't work out all that well, I'm afraid to say.

Step 4: Record and Live by Your Higher Power.

Once you hear from your higher power, record and live by your higher calling. Simple. Easy-peasy!

Mark's Example - Higher Calling

Let's see what Mark does with this Higher Calling:

Step 1. Believe.

In college, Mark heard the gospel for the first time. He learned that there's a Holy God, that the wages of sin is death, and Mark knew he was a sinner. But God sent His only Son to die for him, and all who believe can know God and have eternal life. Mark's eyes were opened. The truth was so clear to him. God the Father was and is the Higher Power. Mark gave his life to Him on the spot and believed. He had faith.

Step 2. Pray for Your Calling.

For years, Mark studied the Bible, went to church, and did all of the Christian "things." But he felt like there had to be more. He came across a verse that said, "Find out what you were saved for," and so he started praying, asking God what he was saved for. Over time, he felt God speak to him through the Bible, interactions with other believers, and in his own prayer time that he was to help people as much as he

173

could. When Mark looked around, those people were his wife and kids, the people he worked with, other couples, and he had always had a desire to help orphans. It became clear to Mark that he didn't have to become Superman, but that he could simply help those who were already in his life. He continued to love his family, and he and his wife got involved in marriage ministry. He would teach new PT grads the business to help them succeed as well as be a Christian example for them, and eventually, he and his wife would look into helping orphans.

Step 3. Depend and Trust.

Mark, as an achiever, wasn't very good at this depending on God thing in the beginning. He had been pretty successful in whatever he did, so depending on someone else, even God, was foreign to him. But over time, Mark started to realize that he was pushing his agenda over God's agenda. He began to sit back, pray, and wait for God to act. It was slow and gradual at first. And then it became more and more amazing as the things he had been praying for started happening regularly. Every morning he pauses, prays, and asks God that His will be done, not Mark's. He asks God to show him where He is working today and to give him a nudge if he doesn't notice.

He has taught and helped over 100 PT grads, he and his wife have helped dozens of couples in their town, and just yesterday...just yesterday, he was promoted to general manager of his Physical Therapy practice. And in a couple of months, he and his wife are flying to Africa...to visit their first orphanage. They don't know if it's time or if it's the one, but an uncanny set of circumstances cropped up that they thought could only be their God at work. So they will go over and confirm if that is the case.

Step 4: Record your Higher Calling.

Mark's Higher Calling: Help people in your life as much as you can.

His Higher Calling also happened to be Mark's purpose. Huh. Go figure. Talk about alignment.

And, oh, whether you believe it or not, You *are* God's *masterpiece.* That is one thing Mark believes, as do I.

Recap - Higher Calling

The ultimate way to live a Life that Matters is by embracing a higher calling. It means living a life of trust and dependency on a higher power. You may or may not believe in this, and that's perfectly fine. However, if there's even a small part of your past that involved a higher power, I encourage you to revisit that. If you believe in a higher power but haven't found your calling, I urge you to seek it out—to love the Lord your God with all your heart, soul, and mind. I believe he will reveal it to you.

###

For these tools and additional resources to develop Manifesto #10 & #11, visit www.madetomatter.coach/manifesto.

Epilogue

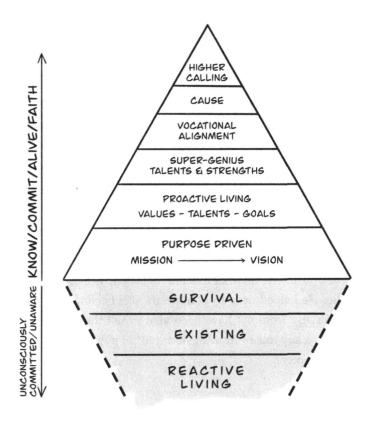

The Life That Matters Manifesto gives you the eleven principles you need to proactively live a Life That Matters. It starts with knowing your Manifesto items, but that's just the beginning. Once you know what you're made of, the next step is to commit to living out what you believe. This will require faith—both in yourself and, for many, in a higher power. When you know, commit, and believe, you come alive. And when you're alive, you can truly live a Life That Matters.

But remember, you already matter—very much. This book is about realizing you matter and proactively living a fulfilled life, a full life, a life of joy, rich relationships, and meaningful accomplishments.

Speaking of accomplishments, let's get an update on Mark's vision.

Mark Epilogue

Mark and Amy ended up having quite a full life. They wrote their marriage book, spoke at conferences, and helped thousands of marriages.

While Mark never wrote a bestseller, he did write five books and immensely enjoyed the process itself.

Mark also built a group of physical therapy practices, though it wasn't as large as his vision had pictured. Still, he made high-seven figures from the deal and retained significant ownership in a large real estate portfolio. He helped over 15 practice owners become millionaires, who otherwise wouldn't have been able to sell their practices. He also played a key role in training hundreds of physical therapists for successful careers.

He and Amy built their dream home almost exactly as they envisioned. They also acquired two other properties—a small, sustainable cabin in the mountains and a large seven-bedroom villa in Italy.

Mark did have a jet for two years, but it turned out to be too expensive, and he didn't use it nearly as much as he thought he would, so he let it go.

Although Mark and Amy had a vision of giving away a million dollars a year, they adjusted that to $100,000 per year after realizing the math didn't support their original goal. Even then, they found it challenging to give away about $275 a day. Often, they would give it weekly, and if they couldn't, they'd write checks to charity. They had many stories of how needs were miraculously met because of their generosity, believing that God used them in this way.

Their kids did marry great spouses, and Mark and Amy helped relieve some of the new spouses' student debt. All nine of their grandchildren went to college debt-free thanks to the 529 college fund matches they provided.

Mark and Amy also adopted an orphanage as their higher calling and cause. It cost about $50,000 per year to fund, making it one of the most well-supported orphanages in Africa. Hundreds of parentless kids who had little hope ended up finding families and a new lease on life because of Mark and Amy. Their Italian villa played a key role in their travels to the orphanage.

Mark didn't quite become the super Christian his vision had imagined, but he did live with faith and dependence, and he loved his God deeply.

In their later years, Mark and Amy looked back at their life with great satisfaction. They lived a fulfilled life, nearly realizing their entire vision. They enjoyed a beautiful family and a strong relationship with God. Their marriage was blessed, and through their lives, they impacted other marriages and the lives of hundreds of kids—not to mention their own children, spouses, and grandchildren. They had great friendships, and Mark transitioned from a job he really enjoyed to a career he absolutely loved. The blessings were truly too many to count.

###

Let's go back to the golfer's visualization analogy. Mark visualized knocking the ball into the hole from 180 yards out. He didn't quite do that. Instead, he knocked it stiff, pin-high, setting up a tap in birdie. Not a bad shot. Not a bad shot at all. Mark's vision helped him achieve a remarkable life.

Next Steps

As I said earlier, Rome wasn't built in a day, and building your Life That Matters Manifesto won't be built in a day either. But don't fret, there are three ways to get help on building your own Manifesto:

Signup for one or several of the following at www.madetomatter.com/manifesto.

1. **Email How-To Series**. Sign-up on our website for a free *11 Principles of The Life That Matters Manifesto Email How-To series*. We will send you an email a week with the appropriate resources for you to do the exercises to develop your Manifesto over 11 weeks. ($$)
2. **Workbook How-To Series (PDF)**. Order the *11 Principles of The Life That Matters Manifesto Workbook* from our website. (Free)
3. **Online Manifesto Course**. Order the multi-part online course on our website. ($$$)
4. **Personal Coaching.** For select clients, I personally coach them around developing their Life That Matters Manifesto over a year coaching program. Contact me through my website. ($$$$$)

Know Your Manifesto items. Commit to living. Come Alive. Have Faith. And achieve a remarkable life. And live a Life That Matters. Here's to the courageous ones who will commit to living a Life That Matters. Godspeed.

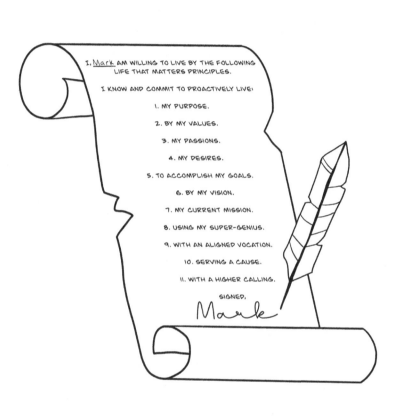

I, Mark AM WILLING TO LIVE BY THE FOLLOWING
LIFE THAT MATTERS PRINCIPLES.

I KNOW AND COMMIT TO PROACTIVELY LIVE:

1. MY PURPOSE.

2. BY MY VALUES.

3. MY PASSIONS.

4. MY DESIRES.

5. TO ACCOMPLISH MY GOALS.

6. BY MY VISION.

7. MY CURRENT MISSION.

8. USING MY SUPER-GENIUS.

9. WITH AN ALIGNED VOCATION.

10. SERVING A CAUSE.

11. WITH A HIGHER CALLING.

SIGNED,

Mark

About the Author

Adam Landrum is an Executive Coach and founder of Made to Matter Coaching, focused on helping individuals in the second-half of their lives to lead with purpose and achieve their dreams. His work centers around offering clarity and direction to those navigating career transitions, defining their organizational roles, or embarking on new ventures. Through personalized coaching, Adam enables his clients to uncover their life's purpose and second-career aspirations, guiding them towards a life filled with greater fulfillment and impact.

Adam received his training from two different coaching bodies, including iPEC and The Conscious Leadership Group. His clients include executives ranging from Fortune 500 companies to successful entrepreneurs and has served executives in sectors that include tech, biomedical, health care, real estate, manufacturing, professional services, and more.

In Adam's early career, he worked for the largest professional service firm in the world at the time, Arthur Andersen, and later became the founder and CEO of Up&Up, a nationally recognized brand and marketing firm exclusively serving universities. He successfully exited the company he founded by selling his firm. He is the author of *The Life That Matters Manifesto: The 11 Principles to Know and Commit to Live a Life That Matters*. He resides in Greenville, SC with his wife, Shely. They are proud parents of their four children.

Please Visit:
www.MadetoMatter.coach/manifesto for more information.
www.linkedin.com/in/adamlandrum/

Printed in the United States
by Baker & Taylor Publisher Services